HOOPER & CO. (COACHBUILDERS) LTD. LONDON

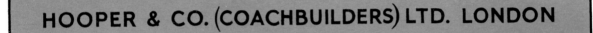

COACHWORK BY   JAMES YOUNG LᵗᴰD   BROMLEY KENT

CHISWICK   H.J. Mulliner & Co., Ltd.   LONDON

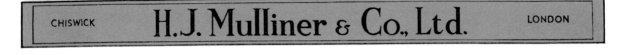

Park-Ward Coachwork

FREESTONE & WEBB LᵗᴰD
101-103, BRENTFIELD ROAD,   WILLESDEN,   N.W. 10.   ELGAR 6671·2·3

─ COACHWORK BY ─
H.J. Mulliner, Park Ward Limited.
─ WILLESDEN LONDON ─

ROLLS-ROYCE, THE ELEGANCE CONTINUES

For sheer elegance, my personal preference is the Phantom V with a James Young Touring Limousine, design PV 23.

ROLLS-ROYCE

THE ELEGANCE CONTINUES

LAWRENCE DALTON

DALTON WATSON LTD

LONDON

First Published 1971
Revised and reprinted 1973

SBN 901564 052

© Lawrence Dalton 1971

Process Engravings by Star Illustration Works Ltd
Printed in England by the Lavenham Press Ltd
for the publishers
DALTON WATSON LTD
76 Wardour Street, London W1V 4AN

Distributed in the U.S.A. by
Motorbooks International
3501 Hennepin Avenue South
Minneapolis
Minnesota 55408

Preface

In continuing the theme of 'Those Elegant Rolls-Royce' into the post-war period, a considerable difficulty immediately presented itself. Whereas for the earlier book there had been a plethora of material from which to draw and in fact only about seven hundred of the two thousand photographs available were used, this time the subject matter was very sparse.

Coachbuilding like many of the crafts is dying, the fifty or more pre-war coachbuilders were reduced by 1946 to under twenty building bodies for Rolls-Royce and of these only six produced any quantity. By 1960, James Young alone survived outside of the Rolls-Royce group, and with the advent of the Silver Shadow they too ceased coachbuilding, leaving only H. J. Mulliner, Park Ward.

A further limiting factor was the relatively small number of different designs each coachbuilder produced; post-war production runs of twenty-five or more were not uncommon, this gave output but not variety.

To counteract this general diminishment, I no longer restricted myself to using solely the rather less flattering profile view of the car and in fact many cars are illustrated in a number of different positions, thereby showing off boots to better advantage. Interior photographs are now included, as are manufacturer's line drawings and designer's wash drawings and, what I personally found to be of the greatest interest, extracts of some of the coachbuilder's body books.

These extracts are published in all good faith as being complete and correct, but whether in fact this is so is hard to elicit. As coachbuilding declined, records seemed to have been neglected and it is possible that some entries were not made. Also the human error creeps in, chassis numbers sometimes have their letters transposed; where this has been noticed, it has been corrected, in one book two entries, one under the other, had the same chassis number, this Rolls-Royce managed partially to solve.

Of course not all the Body Books were identical in the information they provided. H. J. Mulliner, for instance, did not include the design number, this had to be extracted from another source. The Park

Ward post-war book could not be found, although earlier records were available. James Young allocated blocks of numbers to different designs, this causes some confusion when dating cars, i.e. job number 2001 could have been made ten years earlier than job number 1895, and after job number 1899 the number jumped to 9000, but reverted to 4000 on the introduction of the Silver Cloud.

It must be remembered that I have extracted only job numbers referring to coachwork mounted on Rolls-Royce chasses, therefore bodies constructed for Bentley, Daimler, Humber and other makes have been ignored.

One of the endearing factors that made the compilation of this book such a pleasure, was the wholehearted co-operation I received from everyone, anything to do with coachbuilding. From Denis Miller-Williams of Rolls-Royce who let me loot his photographic files for days, from R. Winterton of Jack Barclays who gave me a copy of every photograph they had in the building. From G. F. Moseley of H. J. Mulliner, Park Ward who spent hours on many different days identifying Park Ward, H. J. Mulliner and H. J. Mulliner, Park Ward photographs and supplying with those that were missing. From E. Aylward and F. Fuller who turned James Young inside out in the search for photographs and drawings, from Osmond Rivers with whom a day soon went on matters Hooper, from J. Knott who vetted the Freestone & Webb chapter, and who put me in touch with T. M. A. Elsan of the Science Museum which holds so much Hooper material, from R. T. Malcolm of Henleys, one-time Windovers, who dug into personal files and extracted drawings, and from photographer R. Bowers of 7, Spur Road, Isleworth, Middlesex whose glass negatives, immaculately filed, searched to find Freestone & Webb and Hooper photographs. From the enthusiasts both of this country and of the U.S.A. who wrote offering encouragement, information and photographs.

To all of these and undoubtedly many more I should have mentioned but have not, my sincere thanks, they wrote the book, I put it together.

Contents

Acknowledgment

The author and publishers would like to record their sincere appreciation to the following persons and organisations for supplying the photographs, drawings and certain coachbuilding records and for their permission to reproduce them.

Jack Alpe Ltd., pages 53 bottom, 64 bottom, 108 top, 116 centre and bottom. The Autocar, page 258 bottom, Jack Barclay Ltd., pages 34, 35 bottom, 39 top, 45 top, 47 top, 59 bottom, 79 top, 81 bottom, 82 bottom, 83 bottom, 90 top, 134 top, 135 centre, 137 centre, 143 centre, 146 centre, 149 top, 152 top, 155 top, 162 bottom, 170 top, 176 bottom, 177 bottom, 180 top, 209, 211 bottom, 212 bottom, 213 bottom, 214 top, 215 top, 216 bottom, 217 bottom, 219 top, 220 centre and bottom, 221 centre and bottom, 222 bottom, 224 centre and bottom, 225 top and bottom, 226 top and bottom, 227 bottom, 234 top, 235, 237, 241 top and bottom, 243 top, 244 bottom, 249 bottom, 261 centre. A. C. Bell, Esq., page 263 bottom. Chiltern Cars Ltd., page 263 top, Richard Colton Esq., pages 46, 81 top, 132 centre, 144 bottom, 145. C. Coward Esq., page 58. Frank Dale Ltd., pages 49 bottom, 90 centre and bottom, 100 bottom, 103 top, 135 bottom, 136 centre, 143 top, 189 top. Andrew Darling Esq., page 253 bottom. Derby Corporation page 132 bottom. Bill Dobson Esq., page 92. H. S. Fry Esq., pages 57 bottom, 254. Ghia S.P.A. page 253 top. G. W. Harris Esq., page 261 top and bottom. J. Knott Esq., pages 31, 32, 33. K. G. Langley Esq., page 134 centre and bottom. R. T. Malcolm Esq., page 262. H. R. Owen Ltd., pages 36 bottom, 39 bottom, 55 bottom, 59 top, 61 top, 63 bottom. Richard Riley Esq., page 112 bottom. A. G. Rippey Esq., page 144 top. Rippon Bros. Ltd., pages 258 top, 259 bottom. O. Rivers Esq., pages 67, 68, 69, 70, 71, 72, 73, 74, 75, 76, 77. Rolls-Royce Motors Ltd., pages, 3, 12, 14, 16, 17, 18, 19, 20, 21, 22, 23, 24, 25, 26, 28, 36 top, 37, 38, 40, 44 bottom, 51 top, 78, 82 top, 83 top, 84, 85, 87, 88 top, 91, 93 bottom, 94 top, 95 top, 96, 98, 99, 102 bottom, 103 centre, 104, 105, 108 bottom, 109, 110 top, 113 top, 114, 115, 118, 119, 120, 121, 122, 123, 124, 125, 126, 127, 128, 129, 130, 131, 132 top, 133 top and bottom, 135 top, 136 top and bottom, 137 top and bottom, 138, 139, 140, 141, 142, 143 bottom, 146 top and bottom, 147, 148, 149 centre and bottom, 150, 151, 152 centre and bottom, 153, 154, 155 bottom, 156, 157, 158, 159, 160, 162 top, 163, 164, 165, 166, 167, 168, 169, 170 bottom, 171, 172, 173, 174, 175, 176 top, 177 top and centre, 178, 179, 181, 182, 184, 185, 186, 187, 188, 189 bottom, 190, 191, 192, 193, 194, 210, 211 top, 212 top, 213 top, 214 centre, 215 bottom, 216 top and centre, 217 top, 219 bottom, 220 top, 222 top and centre, 226 centre, 231 bottom, 237 top, 240, 242 top, 246, 247, 248, 255, 256, 257, 259 bottom, 264 top. David Stockwell Esq., pages 49 top, 50 bottom, Dr. Irving Thrasher, page 251, Vincents of Reading Ltd., page 260, A. R. Walsh Esq., page 89 centre, James Young Ltd., pages 197, 198, 199, 200, 201, 202, 203, 204, 205, 206, 207, 208, 214 bottom, 217 centre, 218, 221 top, 223, 224 top, 225 centre, 227 top and centre, 228, 229, 230, 231 top and centre, 232, 233, 234 centre and bottom, 236, 238, 239, 241 centre, 242 centre and bottom, 243 centre and bottom, 244 top, 249 top.

CHAPTER ONE

FROM SILVER WRAITH TO CORNICHE

Although this book is concerned with coachbuilt bodies mounted on post-war Rolls-Royce chassis, the market for such cars has almost entirely disappeared. Anticipating and perhaps encouraging this trend Rolls-Royce began to produce complete motor cars, introducing the Silver Dawn in 1949, although as a company, Rolls-Royce actually started in 1946 with the Mark VI Bentley

This has meant a slight alteration to the format employed in "Those Elegant Rolls-Royce" and this chapter deals with the standard coachwork produced by Rolls-Royce, together with brief chassis specifications of all the following models mentioned in the chapters.

SILVER WRAITH

SILVER DAWN

PHANTOM IV

SILVER CLOUDS

PHANTOM V

SILVER SHADOW

PHANTOM VI

CORNICHE

Chassis numbers and the details of the models have been supplied from the Rolls-Royce records.

SILVER WRAITH

The Silver Wraith chassis.

*Introduced
1946*

*Ceased
production
1959*

Rolls-Royce recommenced motor car production after the war with the Silver Wraith, the first batch of chassis being delivered in late 1946.

During its fourteen years of production the engine size was enlarged from 4257 cc on introduction to 4566 cc in 1951 and again in 1955 to 4887 cc. The chassis started life with a 10 ft. 7 in. wheelbase which was supplemented in 1951 with a long wheelbase version of 11 ft. 1 in., the standard 10 ft. 7 in. chassis then being dropped the next year.

Many devotees of the marque think of the tall, stately Silver Wraith as being the last real Rolls-Royce. This view points out that no later model was mounted with solely specialist coach-work and that these bodies were of a wide range of designs, the work of at least a dozen coachbuilders. This of course discounts the Phantoms V and VI, but the Phantom V certainly had very few different designs and the Phantom VI even less.

Brief Specification

6 cylinder pushrod operated overhead inlet and side exhaust valve engine.

Bore	$3\frac{1}{2}$ ins. enlarged in 1951 to $3\frac{5}{8}$ ins.	
	and in 1955 to $3\frac{3}{4}$ ins.	
Stroke	$4\frac{1}{2}$ ins.	
Capacity	4257 cc, 1951 4566 cc, 1955 4887 cc	
Wheelbase	10 ft. 7 ins. Long wheelbase 11 ft. 1 in.	
Track front	4 ft. 10 ins.	4 ft. 10 ins.
rear	5 ft.	5 ft. 4 ins.
Tyres	6.50 x 17	7.50 x 16

Chassis Numbers

Standard wheelbase
WTA 1-85, WVA 1-81, WYA 1-87
WZB 1-65, WAB 1-65, WCB 1-73
WDC 1-101, WFC 1-101, WGC 1-101
WHD 1-101
WLE 1-35, WME 1-96
WOF 1-76
WSG 1-76
SVH 1-116

Long wheelbase
ALW 1-51
BLW 1-101
CLW 1-43
DLW 1-166
ELW 1-101
FLW 1-101
GLW 1-26
HLW 1-52

The letter L before the three letters of the chassis number denotes a left hand drive car i.e. LWHD 10.
The number 13 was not used.

SILVER DAWN

Introduced
1949

Ceased
production
1955

Introduced particularly with the American market in mind, the Silver Dawn was to all intents and purposes a Mark VI Bentley standard steel Saloon with a Rolls-Royce radiator. The first cars were only available with left hand drive and had a steering column gear lever. In fact very few of what might be termed the small boot Silver Dawn had right hand steering.

In late 1952 the large boot model was introduced having an optional automatic gearbox and by the Earls Court Motor Show of 1953 this model was available in Great Britain.

Because of its compact size the Silver Dawn has always been popular and commanded a high second-hand value. In 1971 the price for examples in good condition is about half of their original £4700 price.

Below: An imposing view of a later Silver Dawn, and opposite, one of the earlier small boot versions which were almost entirely built with left hand drive for the export market.

Brief Specification

6 cylinder pushrod operated overhead inlet and side exhaust valve engine.

Bore $3\frac{1}{2}$ ins. enlarged in 1951 to $3\frac{5}{8}$ ins.

Stroke $4\frac{1}{2}$ ins.

Capacity 4257 cc, 1951 4566 cc

Wheelbase 10 ft.

Track front 4 ft. $8\frac{1}{2}$ ins.

rear 4 ft. $10\frac{5}{8}$ ins.

Tyres 6.50 x 16

Chassis Numbers

SBA 2-138, SCA 1-63

SDB 2-140

SFC 2-160

SHD 2-60

SKE 2-50, SLE 1-51

SMF 2-76, SNF 1-125

SOG 2-100, SPG 1-101

SRH 2-100, STH 1-101

SUJ 2-130, SVJ 1-133

Chassis numbers starting at 1 use only odd numbers and do not use 13, chassis numbers starting at 2 use only even numbers. The letter L before the three letters of the chassis number denotes a left hand driver car i.e. LSVJ 133.

The Silver Dawn standard Saloon as is normally seen in England.

PHANTOM IV

The Phantom IV chassis

Introduced
1950

Ceased
production
1956

Envisaged as a Heads of State model and using the only straight eight cylinder engine yet to have been installed in a production Rolls-Royce car, the Phantom IV predates the long wheelbase Silver Wraith by about a year.

Very limited production over the course of seven years only totalled seventeen motor cars manufactured, this excludes 4 AF4 which was a works test vehicle and subsequently dismantled.

Twelve of the seventeen cars made are illustrated, six in the Hooper chapter and six in the H. J. Mulliner, one that unfortunately no photograph of which was forthcoming is 4 AF22, an Allweather body by Franay, delivered to Prince Talal Al Saoud Ryak of Saudi Arabia. No other coachbuilder mounted a body on a Phantom IV chassis save the three just named.

Brief Specification

8 cylinder in line engine with pushrod operated overhead inlet and side exhaust valves.

Bore	3½ ins.
Stroke	4½ ins.
Capacity	5675 cc
Wheelbase	12 ft. 1 in.
Track front	4 ft. 10½ ins.
rear	5 ft. 3 ins.
Tyres	7.00 x 17

Chassis Numbers

4 AF2 — 4 AF22 even numbers
4 BP1 — 4 BP7 odd numbers
4 CS2 — 4 CS 6 even numbers

View showing the massive cross-braced chassis and twin exhaust system.

SILVER CLOUD I, II, III

The Silver Cloud chassis.

Introduced
1955

Silver Cloud III
ceased production
1966

The advent in 1955 of the Silver Cloud and the Bentley 'S' Series standard steel Saloons must rank among the most important reasons why most of the few remaining coachbuilders ceased to produce bodies for Rolls-Royce and Bentley chassis.

The Silver Dawn standard Saloon, being a Rolls-Royce radiatored Bentley, had not greatly impinged on the Silver Wraith market. However the Silver Cloud, with the Silver Wraith track and a longer wheelbase than the Silver Dawn, mounted with a beautifully proportioned body was an entirely different adversary. Here now was a car that looked so right but cost much less than a chassis mounted with specialist coachwork, that in 1958 Freestone & Webb ceased coachbuilding, followed a year later by Hooper. Even Rolls-Royce themselves merged their two coachbuilding interests into one unit.

If anything detrimental can be said about the Silver Clouds, forgetting the slight rust problem, it must be that one can have too much of a good thing.

The standard Saloon was cut and lengthened by Park Ward for the long wheelbase cars and at H. J. Mulliner they converted the four door Saloon into a delightful two door Drophead Coupé.

The Silver Cloud standard steel Saloon. Below: the Silver Cloud long wheelbase standard steel Saloon. The standard Saloon body was cut and lengthened by Park Ward.

Brief Specification

Silver Cloud I

6 cylinder pushrod operated overhead inlet and side exhaust valve engine.

Bore	$3\frac{3}{4}$ ins.		
Stroke	$4\frac{1}{2}$ ins.		
Capacity	4887 cc		
Wheelbase	10 ft. 3 ins.	Long wheelbase	10 ft. 7 ins.
Track front	4 ft. 10 ins.		4 ft. 10 ins.
rear	5 ft.		5 ft.
Tyres	8.20 x 15		8.20 x 15

The Silver Cloud III standard steel Saloon. Below: the long wheelbase version.

Brief Specification	Silver Clouds II & III

90 degree V8, pushrod operated overhead valve engine.

Bore	4.1 ins.		
Stroke	3.6 ins.		
Capacity	6230 cc		
Wheelbase	10 ft. 3 ins.	Long wheelbase	10 ft. 7 ins.
Track front	4 ft. 10½ ins.		4 ft. 10½ ins.
rear	5 ft.		5 ft.
Tyres	8.20 x 15		8.20 x 15

Chassis Numbers

Silver Cloud I—Standard wheelbase   Long wheelbase
SWA 2-250, SXA 1-251   ALC 1-26
SYB 2-250, SZB 1-251   BLC 1-51
SBC 2-150, SCC 1-151   CLC 1-47
SDD 2-450, SED 1-451
SFE 1-501, SGE 2-500
SHF 1-249, SJF 2-250
SKG 1-125, SLG 2-126
SMH 1-265, SNH 2-262

Silver Cloud II—Standard wheelbase Long wheelbase
SPA 2-326, SRA 1-325   LCA 1-76
STB 2-500, SVB 1-501   LCB 1-101
SWC 2-730, SXC 1-671   LCC 1-101
SYD 2-550, SZD 1-551   LCD 1-25
SAE 1-685

Silver Cloud III—Standard wheelbase Long wheelbase
SAZ 1-61   CAL 1-83
SCX 1-877   CBL 1-61
SDW 1-601   CCL 1-101
SEV 1-495   CDL 1-95
SFU 1-803   CEL 1-105
SGT 1-659   CFL 1-41
SHS 1-357   CGL 1-29
SJR 1-623
SKP 1-423
CSC 1B—CSC 141B
LCSC 1C—CSC 19C

On standard wheelbase Silver Cloud I and II, chassis numbers starting at 1 use only odd numbers, chassis numbers starting at 2 use only even numbers.

The number 13 was not used.

The letter L before the three letters of the chassis number denotes a left hand drive car i.e. LSLG 110.

Below: the Silver Cloud III chassis

PHANTOM V

The prototype Phantom V with a test rig body.

Introduced
1959

Ceased
production
1968

With the introduction of the Phantom V, lesser mortals than Heads of States were again able to buy a Phantom, the first for twenty years. It superseded the long wheelbase Silver Wraith and by adding twelve inches to the Silver Wraith's wheelbase it provided a magnificent base for the best the coachbuilders could produce.

Unfortunately by now there were very few coachbuilders and possibly the most notable of all, Hoopers, was to close having mounted but one body on the Phantom V chassis. However James Young took up the challenge and their Touring Limousines on the Phantom V chassis are some of the most elegant closed cars ever built.

Brief Specification

90 degree V8, pushrod operated overhead valve engine.

Bore	4.1 ins.	Track front	5 ft. $0\frac{7}{8}$ ins.
Stroke	3.6 ins.	rear	5 ft. 4 ins.
Capacity	6230 cc	Tyres	8.90 x 15
Wheelbase	12 ft. 1 in.		

Chassis Numbers

5 AS 1-101
5 AT 2-100
5 BV 1-101
5 BX 2-100
5 CG 1-79

Chassis numbers starting at 1 use only odd numbers, chassis numbers starting at 2 use only even numbers.

5 VA 1-123
5 VB 1-51
5 VC 1-51
5 VD 1-101
5 VE 1-51
5 VF 1-183

The number 13 was not used.

The letter L before the two letters of the chassis number denotes a left hand drive car.

The Phantom V chassis.

SILVER SHADOW

The Silver Shadow standard Saloon.

Introduced 1966

The chassisless Silver Shadow with its stressed steel monocoque body was an entirely new motor car, owing nothing to the Silver Clouds save its engine.

Here was a four door Saloon with a smaller wheelbase and track, with independent suspension on all wheels and disc brakes, and with no chassis on which the specialist coachbuilders could build.

James Young modified fifty standard four-door saloons into two door saloons and then quit coachbuilding, leaving H. J. Mulliner, Park Ward as the only remaining coachbuilder constructing bodies for Rolls-Royce motor cars.

A long wheelbase model was introduced in 1969, and the engine was enlarged to 6750 cc in 1971.

Brief Specification

90 degree V8 pushrod operated overhead valve engine.

Bore	4.1 ins.	
Stroke	3.6 ins. enlarged in 1971 to 3.9 ins.	
Capacity	6230 cc, 1971 6750 cc.	
Wheelbase	9 ft. 11½ ins.	Long wheelbase 10 ft. 3½ ins.
Track front	4 ft. 9½ ins.	4 ft. 9½ ins.
rear	4 ft. 9½ ins.	4 ft. 9½ ins.
Tyres	8.45 x 15	8.45 x 15

Below: the Silver Shadow Limousine with lengthened wheelbase.

PHANTOM VI

The Phantom VI

*Introduced
1968*

The Earls Court Motor Show of 1968 saw the introduction of the Phantom VI, a Phantom V in all but detail.

The overall dimensions were identical, but the more powerful Shadow engine was used against the Cloud III engine of the Phantom V. The new car also had full air conditioning installed for both front and rear compartments, supplied by separate units in the scuttle and luggage boot.

Brief Specification

90 degree V8, pushrod operated overhead valve engine.

Bore	4.1 ins.	Track front	5 ft. $0\frac{7}{8}$ ins.
Stroke	3.6 ins.	rear	5 ft. 4 ins.
Capacity	6230 cc	Tyres	8.90 x 15
Wheelbase	12 ft. 1 in.		

CORNICHE

The Corniche Drop-head Coupé.

Introduced
1971

The Silver Shadow with the H. J. Mulliner, Park Ward Fixed-head and Drop-head Coupé bodies have now been given a model designation. These two bodies have been illustrated in the H.J.M., P.W. chapter so it is really pointless to show them again, but in case it is said the book is incomplete, the Drop-head Coupé with the hood stowed is shown.

Bodily there is no difference between the Silver Shadow Coupés and the Corniche except for minor modifications, the engine however is a more powerful version of the new enlarged engine installed in the Silver Shadow.

Brief Specification

90 degree V8 pushrod operated overhead valve engine.

Bore	4.1 ins.
Stroke	3.9 ins.
Capacity	6750 cc
Wheelbase	9 ft. $11\frac{1}{2}$ ins.
Track front	4 ft. $9\frac{1}{2}$ ins.
rear	4 ft. $9\frac{1}{2}$ ins.
Tyres	205 x 15

CHAPTER TWO

FREESTONE AND WEBB

The coachbuilding firm of Freestone and Webb was formed in 1923 by V. E. Freestone and A. J. Webb for the sole purpose of car body building. Mr. Freestone was from Crossley Motors, and Mr. Webb came from a French firm of coachbuilders. Its workshops were at Brentfield Road, Willesden, London, which was its only home during its existence as an independent company. They concentrated on building bodies to private order on Rolls-Royce and Bentley chassis, output on the Rolls-Royce eventually averaging some fifteen a year.

One of the body designs developed by Freestone and Webb became known as the Top Hat. The firm also had a hand in popularising the "razor edge" style.

During World War II the company switched to aircraft production, working mainly on Spitfire wing tips.

Freestone and Webb exhibited regularly at the London Motor Show, and for nine consecutive years won the Gold Medal in the Private Coachbuilders competition.

On the death of A. J. Webb in 1955 the company was taken over by H. R. Owen Ltd., of Berkeley Street, London, W.1, part of the Swain Group, but continued to build bodies only until 1958.

Extracts from
Freestone & Webb
body book
referring to coachwork
mounted on Rolls-Royce
chassis only

BODY NO	DESIGN NO	CHASSIS	CHASSIS NO	TYPE OF BODY	REMARKS
1354	3004/1	Silver Wraith	WTA37	4D 4L Brougham Sal.	
1357	3004/A3	Silver Wraith	WVA72	4D 4L Sal. Lim.	Off B1354
1383	3005	Silver Wraith	WTA44	4D 4L Touring Body	
1384	3014	Silver Wraith	WVA74	2D 4L F/H Coupé	Special Design
1385	3004	Silver Wraith	WVA53	4D 4L Saloon	Off B1354
1391	3004/A2	Silver Wraith	WVA21	4D 6L Sal. Lim.	Off B1354
1392	3004/C	Silver Wraith	WYA16	4D 4L Sal. Lim.	Wheels at side of bonnet
1393	3004/A	Silver Wraith	WYA4	4D 4L Sal. Lim.	Off B1354
1394	3004/A	Silver Wraith	WVA81	4D 4L Sal. Lim.	Off B1354
1398	3004/A	Silver Wraith	WVA19	4D 4L Sal. Lim.	Off B1354
1416	3004	Silver Wraith	WZB55	4D 6L Saloon	Doors Front Hinged
1418	3004	Silver Wraith	WZB25	4D 4L Sal. Lim.	As B1354
1422	3004/B	Silver Wraith	WAB12	4D 4L Saloon	As B1354
1424	3004/A	Silver Wraith	WYA84	4D 4L Limousine	As B1354
1426	3004	Silver Wraith	WYA62	4D 4L Saloon	As B1354
1429	3004	Silver Wraith	WZB42	4D 4L Saloon	As B1354
1430	3004	Silver Wraith	WYA68	4D 4L Sal. Lim.	As B1354
1432	3004/A	Silver Wraith	WYA74	4D 4L Sal. Lim.	As B1354
1435	3004/B	Silver Wraith	WAB46	4D 4L Saloon	Off B1354 Mods. as 1459
1438	3047/B	Silver Wraith	WFC89	4D 6L Saloon	Off 1506
1440	3004/B	Silver Wraith	WZB19	4D 4L Saloon	
1454	3004/2	Silver Wraith	WDC72	4D 6L Saloon	As 1475
1459	3004/B	Silver Wraith	WZB37	4D 4L Saloon	Off 1354 with mods.
1464	3004/A2	Silver Wraith	WDC34	4D 6L Sal. Lim.	As 1475 with mods.
1467	3004/2	Silver Wraith	WCB7	4D 6L Saloon	As 1354 with mods.
1468	3004/A2	Silver Wraith	WFC46	4D 6L Sal. Lim.	Off 1506
1473	3004/B	Silver Wraith	WAB65	4D 4L Saloon	As 1475
1475	3004/A2/F	Silver Wraith	WCB11	4D 6L Sal. Lim.	Off 1354 with mods.
1482	3004/C	Silver Wraith	WDC39	4D 4L Sal. Lim.	As 1475
1487	3047/2A	Silver Wraith	WFC7	4D 6L Saloon	Off 1506
1494	3047/1	Silver Wraith	WDC88	4D 4L Sal. Lim.	Off 1506
1500	3047	Silver Wraith	WVA75	4D 6L Sal. Lim.	As 1475
1502	3050	Silver Wraith	WFC68	4D 6L Sal. Lim.	Special Drawing
1506	3047/2A	Silver Wraith	WDC94	4D 6L Sal. Lim.	New Drawing
1508	3047/2B	Silver Wraith	WZB54	4D 6L Saloon	Off 1506 with mods.
1510	3050	Silver Wraith	WFC32	4D 6L Sal. Lim.	As 1502
1511	3056	Silver Wraith	WFC69	2D 4L D/H Coupé	
1513	3050/A/B	Silver Wraith	WGC19	4D 6L Sal. Lim.	Off 1502 Earls Court Show 1949
1523	3050/A/B	Silver Wraith	WGC50	4D 6L Limousine	As 1513 Off 1502
1524	3050/B	Silver Wraith	WGC99	4D 6L Saloon	Off 1502
1525	3050/A/B	Silver Wraith	WHD15	4D 6L Limousine	Off 1502
1526	3050/B	Silver Wraith	WHD27	4D 6L Saloon	Off 1502
1539	3070/B	Silver Wraith	WHD44	4D 4L Sal. Lim.	As lines of PW '49 Show Job
1541	3068	Silver Wraith	LWHD73	4D 6L Utility Body	New Drawing
1543	3070/A	Silver Wraith	WHD86	4D 4L Sal. Lim.	1539 Modified E.C. Show 1950
1544	3050/A/B	Silver Wraith	WHD76	4D 6L Sal. Lim.	Off 1502 Earls Court Show 1950
1547	3047/B	Silver Wraith	WHD72	4D 6L Saloon	As 1506 no div.
1549	3070	Silver Wraith	WLE29	4D 4L Saloon	Off 1543 no div.

FREESTONE & WEBB

BODY NO	DESIGN NO	CHASSIS	CHASSIS NO	TYPE OF BODY	REMARKS
1567	3070/A	Silver Wraith	WLE20	4D 4L Saloon	Off 1543
1571	3087	Silver Wraith	WOF54	2D 4L F/H/Coupé	FH on sep. drg., use with B1511
1573	3091/A	Silver Wraith	WOF51	4D 6L Limousine	
1574	3092	Silver Wraith	WOF65	4D 6L Saloon	As 1609
1575	3074/A/B	Silver Wraith	WME15	4D 6L 7 Seater Lim.	New drawing
1577	3081	Silver Wraith	WLE27	4D 6L Sal. Lim.	New drawing
1578	3070	Silver Wraith	WOF21	4D 4L Saloon	As 1543 (Rear 1609)
1583	3074/A/B	Silver Wraith	WME40	4D 6L 7 Seater Lim.	As 1575
1587	3050/A/B/C/E	Silver Wraith	WME88	4D 6L Limousine	Off 1502
1589	3070/E	Silver Wraith	WOF41	4D 4L Saloon	
1593	3091/A	Silver Wraith	WSG62	4D 6L Sal. Lim.	Off 1610
1595	3050/A/B/C	Silver Wraith	WOF53	4D 6L Limousine	Off 1502
1601	3091	Silver Wraith	WOF37	4D 6L Saloon	On 1502
1609	3092	Silver Wraith	WOF2	4D 6L Saloon	Earls Court Show 1951
1610	3091/A	Silver Wraith	WOF3	4D 6L Sal. Lim.	Mods. on 1502 E.C. Show 1951
1615	3070/A	Silver Wraith	WVA70	4D 4L Sal. Lim.	Off 1543
1616	3070/A	Silver Wraith	WME52	4D 4L Sal. Lim.	Off 1543
1617	3092	Silver Wraith	WOF58	4D 6L Saloon	As 1609
1626	3050/A/B/C/D	Silver Wraith	WME86	4D 6L Limousine	
1632	3070/A	Silver Wraith	WVH17	4D 4L Sal. Div.	
1636	3092	Silver Wraith	WVH64	4D 6L Saloon	As 1609
1646	3110/A	Silver Wraith	ALW39	4D 6L Limousine	Special Drawing
1654	3092/A	Silver Wraith	WSG2	4D 6L Saloon with Div.	
1663	3087	Silver Wraith	WVH42	2D 4L F/H Coupé	As B1571
1671	3092	Silver Wraith	WVH49	4D 6L Saloon	
1691	3107	Silver Wraith	WVH22	2D 4L F/H Coupé	
1695	3107	Silver Wraith	WVH6	2D 4L F/H Coupé	Earls Court Show 1952
1697	3091/A	Silver Wraith	WVH5	4D 6L Sal. Lim.	Earls Court Show 1952
1708	3092	Silver Wraith	WSG70	4D 6L Saloon	Special P. Bumpers
1709	3110/A	Silver Wraith	ALW33	4D 6L 7 Seater Lim.	Special P. Bumpers
1714	3092	Silver Wraith	WVH44	4D 6L Saloon	
1717	3091	Silver Wraith	WVH58	4D 6L Saloon	
1719	3131/A	Silver Wraith	ALW42	4D 6L Sal. Lim.	
1721	3091/A	Silver Wraith	WVH98	4D 6L Sal. Lim.	
1724	3131/A/L	Silver Wraith	BLW59	4D 6L Sal. Lim.	Earls Court Show 1953
1725	3110/A/L	Silver Wraith	BLW58	4D 6L Limousine	Earls Court Show 1953
1728	3092/A	Silver Wraith	WVH100	4D 6L Sal. Lim.	
1729	3091/A	Silver Wraith	WVH105	4D 6L Sal. Lim.	
1735	3171/A	Silver Wraith	DLW134	4D 6L Limousine	
1739	3131/A/L	Silver Wraith	BLW96	4D 6L Sal. Lim.	
1740	3163	Silver Dawn	SNF107	4D 6L Saloon	P. Bumpers
1743	3170/A	Silver Wraith	DLW8	4D 6L 7 Seater Lim.	
1744	3165	Silver Dawn	SOG46	4D 6L Saloon	3082/C Design
1745	3160	Silver Wraith	LCLW9	4D 4L Concealed Hd.	
1746	3131/A/L	Silver Wraith	CLW31	4D 6L Sal. Lim.	
1747	3171/A	Silver Wraith	CLW32	4D 6L Sal. Lim.	
1749	3131/A/L	Silver Wraith	BLW93	4D 6L Sal. Lim.	
1750	3131/A/L	Silver Wraith	CLW12	4D 6L Sal. Lim.	

BODY NO	DESIGN NO	CHASSIS	CHASSIS NO	TYPE OF BODY	REMARKS
1752	3131/A/L	Silver Wraith	DLW69	4D 6L Sal. Lim.	
1753	3183	Silver Wraith	CLW39	2D 4L F/H Coupé	Special drawing
1754	3131/L	Silver Wraith	CLW37	4D 6L Saloon	
1755	3163	Silver Dawn	SOG50	4D 6L Saloon	
1757	3163	Silver Dawn	SOG48	4D 6L Saloon	
1758	3131/A/L	Silver Wraith	LCLW34	4D 6L Sal. Lim.	
1759	3192/A	Silver Wraith	DLW45	4D 4L Sal. Lim.	S/Dawn Radiator Special Bonnet
1760	3171/A	Silver Wraith	DLW44	4D 6L Limousine	Earls Court Show 1954
1761	3131/A/L/3	Silver Wraith	DLW43	4D 6L Sal. Lim.	Earls Court Show 1954
1764	3190	Silver Wraith	DLW83	4D 6L 7 Seater Lim.	
1765	3163	Silver Dawn	STH53	4D 6L Saloon	
1766	3163	Silver Dawn	STH55	4D 6L Saloon	
1769	3171	Silver Wraith	DLW72	4D 6L Saloon	
1772	3171/A	Silver Wraith	DLW94	4D 6L Limousine	
1774	3171	Silver Wraith	DLW154	4D 6L Saloon	
1776	3171/A	Silver Wraith	DLW138	4D 6L Limousine	
1778	3171/A	Silver Wraith	DLW137	4D 6L Limousine	
1781	3131/A/L	Silver Wraith	DLW160	4D 6L Limousine	
1782	3206	Silver Cloud	SWA56	4D 6L Saloon	Special Rear Seat
1785	3131/A/L	Silver Wraith	ELW8	4D 6L Sal. Lim.	Earls Court Show 1955
1787	3171/A	Silver Wraith	ELW3	4D 6L Limousine	Earls Court Show 1955
1789	3171/A	Silver Wraith	ELW33	4D 6L Limousine	
1790	3171/A	Silver Wraith	ELW57	4D 6L Limousine	
1791	3194	Silver Cloud	SXA49	4D 6L Saloon	
1796	3193	Silver Cloud	SWA42	2D 4L Saloon	
1797	3194	Silver Cloud	SWA48	4D 6L Saloon	
1800	3206	Silver Cloud	SWA74	4D 6L Saloon	
1804	3210/A	Silver Cloud	SWA108	2D 2L F/H Coupé	
1805	3206	Silver Cloud	SZB149	4D 6L Saloon	
1807	3206	Silver Cloud	SXA117	4D 6L Saloon	
1809	3206	Silver Cloud	SXA123	4D 6L Saloon	
1811	3206	Silver Cloud	SYB20	4D 6L Saloon	
1813	3222	Silver Wraith	FLW26	4D 6L 8 Seater Lim.	
1814	3224/S/C	Silver Cloud	SYB24	4D 6L Saloon	
1815	3206	Silver Cloud	SZB95	4D 6L Saloon	Earls Court Show 1956
1816	3171/A	Silver Wraith	FLW8	4D 6L Sal. Lim.	Earls Court Show 1956
1818	3225	Silver Wraith	FLW25	4D 6L 8 Seater Lim.	Earls Court Show 1956
1820	3171/M	Silver Wraith	FLW76	4D 6L Sal. Lim.	
1821	3171/A	Silver Wraith	FLW/77	4D 6L Sal. Lim.	
1822	3230	Silver Wraith	FLW68	4D 6L Sal. Lim.	New Design
1824	3171/A	Silver Wraith	FLW94	4D 6L Limousine	Earls Court Show 1957
1826	3191	Silver Cloud	ALC1	4D 6L Limousine	Earls Court Show 1957
1827	3243/C	Silver Cloud	SED179	2D 2 Str. D/H Coupé	Earls Court Show 1957
1828	3206	Silver Cloud	SED337	4D 6L Saloon	
1829	3191	Silver Cloud	ALC10	4D 6L Limousine	
1830	3225	Silver Wraith	HLW11	4D 6L Limousine	
1833	3243/C	Silver Cloud	SGE270	2D 2 Str. D/H Coupé	

Silver Wraith, WTA 44, with the first Allweather body by Freestone & Webb, mounted on a post war Rolls-Royce chassis, body No. 1383, design No. 3005.

Below: Saloon Limousine with side mounted spare wheels on Silver Wraith, WYA 16, body No. 1392, design No. 3004/C.

Two more design No. 3004 showing how the basic design differed on almost every car, the above car having doors hinged back and front, most bodies of this design had rear hinged doors. Rear wheel spats ranged from the non existant to the totally enclosed. Both are on Silver Wraith chassis, the above is not positively identified, the lower is WVA 19, body No. 1398. Registration No. SMG 720.

Two views of the 1948 Earls Court Show car, again a 3004 design, this time having modified mudguards and what will be termed as the Hooper quarter light. This feature was used by most of the coachbuilders at one time or another but Hoopers first post war body had it and they continued using it until 1958. Saloon Limousine on Silver Wraith, WCB 11, body No. 1475, design No. 3004/A-2/F.

An early 3004 design with Hooper quarter light, this time with a rather flamboyant motif on the rear spats. It is identified as being an early car by the lack of moulding under the window and by the parallel lines of the chromium strip. It is thought to be body No. 1391 on Silver Wraith, WLA 21.

Two views of another design No. 3004, similar to the 1948 show car, a Saloon Limousine. Body No. 1464 on Silver Wraith, WDC 34.

Four door four light Saloon Limousine on Silver Wraith, WDC 88, body No. 1494, design No. 3047/1. Very similar externally to design No. 3004.

Below: Seven seater Limousine with similar mudguarding to above car. Body No. 1575, design No. 3074/A/B on Silver Wraith, WME 15.

Six light Saloon Limousine, exhibited at Earls Court 1949, on Silver Wraith, WGC 19, body No. 1513, design No. 3050/A/B. Very little visible difference to the previous year's show car except for alteration to the rear quarter lights and repositioning of the side lights.

Below: Registration No. ANN 1, thought to be body No. 1502, identical to the 1949 show car except for the side lights being in the 3004 position.

Design 3050 twice more, the upper car Registration No. OLD 8 with basketwork sides and bottom of front doors swept forward. Below: Thought to be a 1950 show car, and if so, it is Silver Wraith, WHD 76, body No. 1544. This photograph was taken in September 1950 and was used in the 'Autocar' description of the show.

Drop-head Coupé with rear quarter lights, body No. 1511, design No. 3056 on Silver Wraith, WFC 69.

Four door six light Saloon Limousine on a Silver Wraith chassis, design No. 3091/A, photograph and coachbuilder's drawing.

Below: Utility body on Silver Wraith, WHD 73, body No. 1541, design No. 3068. Note three rows of seats. The only Freestone & Webb utility body listed.

Body No. 1539, a four door four light Saloon Limousine on Silver Wraith, WHD 44, design No. 3070/B from which the design below is a natural development. Design No. 3092, six light Saloon shown at the 1951 Earls Court Show, body No. 1609 on Silver Wraith, WOF 2.

Six light Saloon on the Silver Wraith chassis, design No. 3092. Photograph and Coachbuilder's drawing.

FREESTONE & WEBB

Two door, four light Fixed Head Coupé on Silver Wraith, WOF 54, body No. 1571, design No. 3087, registration No. 528 GNV, owned by Richard Colton Esq.

Two door four light Fixed Head
Coupé on Silver Wraith, WVH
6, body No. 1695, design No.
3107. Exhibited at the 1952
Earls Court Show.

Two photographs of a 7 seater Limousine, body No. 1646, design No. 3110/A on Silver Wraith, ALW 39.

Listed by Freestone & Webb as four door four light Concealed Head, this body No. 1745, design No. 3160, was originally mounted on Silver Wraith, LCLW 9, but now is on WLE 47. The present owner is David Stockwell Esq.

Below: Two door four light Fixed Head Coupé on Silver Wraith, CLW 39, body No. 1753, design No. 3183.

Design No. 3131 A/L, Coachbuilder's drawing.

Below: Six light Saloon Limousine on Silver Wraith, ALW 42, body No. 1719, design No. 3131/A. Present Owner is David Stockwell Esq. This is the first illustration of the Freestone & Webb special bumper. It is much deeper than the Rolls-Royce bumper and has a very flat appearance.

Two more 3131/A/L designs on Silver Wraith chassis. Again on the lower car note the flat bumper. As later Freestone & Webb and Hooper designs are very similar, the FW flat bumper and the Hooper rear quarter lights, help quick recognition.

Design No. 3163, on the Silver Dawn Chassis, a similar design was mounted on the Silver Wraith chassis and these were a natural development of design No. 3131 A/L.

A seven seater Limousine, body No. 1725, design No. 3110 A/L on Silver Wraith, BLW 58.

Below: Body No. 1764, a 7 seater Limousine on Silver Wraith, DLW 83, design No. 3190.

The 1954 Earls Court Show Limousine on Silver Wraith, DLW 44, body No. 1760, design No. 3171/A. The same look as the Silver Dawn but much more massive.

The Coachbuilder's drawing of design No. 3171/A and another Silver Wraith with same design body this time on chassis FLW 77, body No. 1821.

A four door four light Saloon Limousine, body No. 1759, design No. 3192/A, on Silver Wraith, DLW 45. With a Silver Dawn radiator and a special bonnet, this is a one car design number.

FREESTONE & WEBB

The Silver Cloud carrying on the theme from the Silver Dawn and Silver Wraith, chassis No. SYB 20, body No. 1811, design No. 3206. Eight bodies of this design were built.

A two door version of the car on the previous page. Silver Cloud, SWA 42, body No. 1796, design No. 3193, a two door four light Saloon owned by C. Coward Esq.

Design drawing and photograph of design No. 3224 SC, body No. 1814 on Silver Cloud, SYB 24, a four door six light Saloon of which only one was made.

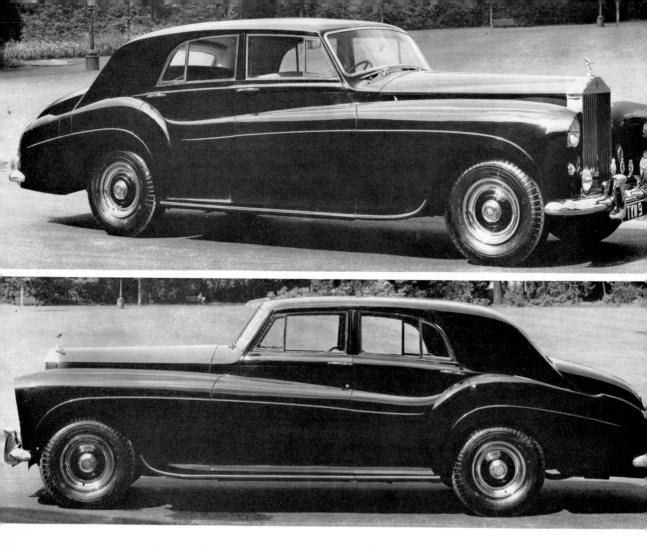

Although I originally thought this car to be a *Silver Cloud* with a modified design
No. 3191 body, it has been pointed out that it has certain *Silver Wraith* features. This
makes identification no easier as there are no four light bodies on late *Silver Wraiths* listed.
Possibly it is body No. 1822 for although in the body book it is listed as a six light, it also
does remark that it is a new design.

Exhibited at the 1957 Earls Court Show, this four-door six light Limousine is on Silver Cloud, ALC 1, body No. 1826, design No. 3191. A sister body was mounted on chassis No. ALC 10.

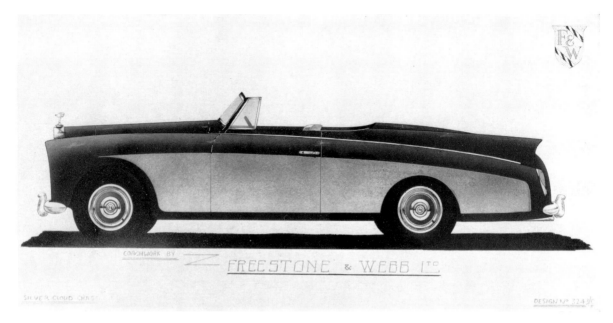

A Show Stopper of 1957, the 2 seater Drop-head Coupé on Silver Cloud, SED 179, body No. 1827, design No. 3243C, which was exhibited on the Freestone & Webb stand at Earls Court in 1957. It is at present owned by John Wise Esq.

Freestone & Webb's penultimate Rolls-Royce body, a four door six light Limousine on Silver Wraith, HLW 11, body No. 1830, design No. 3225, the only car of this design. This car is often seen in London bearing CD plates.

CHAPTER THREE

HOOPER

Hooper, perhaps more than any other coachbuilding firm, founded their considerable reputation on royal patronage. Established in 1805, with premises in the Haymarket, London, they held royal warrants to the British Sovereigns in an unbroken sequence from 1830 when the first one was granted until they closed down after the Second World War.

With a hundred years' experience of coachbuilding behind them, Hoopers readily adapted themselves to the motor age. One of their early commissions was to build a body on a Daimler chassis for King Edward VII in 1904.

By this time Hoopers & Co. (Coachbuilders) Ltd. had established showrooms at the top of St. James' Street in London's West End, and their coachbuilding factory at Chelsea was the biggest of its kind in London.

Between the two World Wars Hoopers were large exporters of specialised bodies. Their clients included the Emperor of Japan, the King of Egypt and the Shah of Persia. Hoopers list of royal and distinguished patrons was, as the Times said at the time, "unequalled by any other coachbuilder in the world".

During the Second World War the firm was taken over by B.S.A., through whom they affected a connection with Daimler, which was then part of B.S.A.

After the war Hoopers restarted coachbuilding, and one of their earliest orders was to build a convertible body for the King of Arabia on a pre-war Phantom III chassis.

They exhibited three models at the 1959 Motor Show, but these were in the nature of a swan song. The models were never repeated, and that year Hoopers ceased finally to make coachwork for "royal and distinguished patrons".

Extracts from
Hooper body book
referring to coachwork
mounted on Rolls-Royce
chassis only

BODY NO	DATE OF DELIVERY	TYPE OF BODY	DESIGN NO	CHASSIS	CHASSIS NO	REMARKS
9173	May 1946	Touring Limousine	8034	Silver Wraith	34G8	
9174	Dec. 1947	Sedanca de Ville	8057	Silver Wraith	WTA71	As 9173
9226	Nov. 1946	Touring Limousine	8034	Silver Wraith	WTA3	As 9173
9227	July 1946	Touring Limousine	8034	Silver Wraith	WTA2	As 9173
9228	Feb. 1947	Touring Limousine	8034	Silver Wraith	WTA6	As 9173
9229	Apr. 1947	Saloon	8060	Silver Wraith	WTA5	As 9173
9230	Mar. 1947	Saloon	8060	Silver Wraith	WTA28	As 9173
9231	Apr. 1947	Touring Limousine	8034	Silver Wraith	WTA10	As 9173
9232	Jan. 1947	Touring Limousine	8034	Silver Wraith	WTA20	No chromium moulding
9233	Apr. 1947	Touring Limousine	8034	Silver Wraith	WTA17	As 9173
9234	Feb. 1947	Touring Limousine	8034	Silver Wraith	WTA7	As 9173 Geneva Show
9235	Apr. 1947	Touring Limousine	8034	Silver Wraith	WTA12	As 9173
9236	Apr. 1947	Touring Limousine	8034	Silver Wraith	WTA26	As 9173
9237	May 1947	Touring Limousine	8034	Silver Wraith	WTA27	As 9173
9238	July 1947	Saloon	8060	Silver Wraith	WTA73	As 9173
9239	May 1947	Touring Limousine	8034	Silver Wraith	WTA8	As 9173
9240	May 1947	Touring Limousine	8034	Silver Wraith	WTA35	As 9173
9241	June 1947	Touring Limousine	8034	Silver Wraith	WTA39	As 9173
9242	Aug. 1947	Saloon	8060	Silver Wraith	WVA34	As 9173
9243	June 1947	Touring Limousine	8034	Silver Wraith	WTA38	As 9173
9244	July 1947	Touring Limousine	8034	Silver Wraith	WTA54	As 9173
9245	July 1947	Touring Limousine	8034	Silver Wraith	WTA70	As 9173
9246	July 1947	Touring Limousine	8034	Silver Wraith	WTA50	As 9173
9247	June 1947	Touring Limousine	8034	Silver Wraith	WTA55	As 9173
9248	June 1947	Touring Limousine	8034	Silver Wraith	WTA56	As 9173
9249	July 1947	Touring Limousine	8034	Silver Wraith	WTA68	As 9173
9250	July 1947	Touring Limousine	8034	Silver Wraith	WTA47	As 9173
9251	July 1947	Touring Limousine	8034	Silver Wraith	WTA76	As 9173
9252	June 1947	Touring Limousine	8034	Silver Wraith	WTA63	As 9173
9253	Aug. 1947	Touring Limousine	8034	Silver Wraith	WTA83	As 9173
9254	Aug. 1947	Touring Limousine	8034	Silver Wraith	WVA2	As 9172
9255	July 1947	Touring Limousine	8034	Silver Wraith	WTA85	As 9173
9256	Dec. 1946	Limousine	8056	Silver Wraith	WTA14	As 9173
9257	Nov. 1947	Saloon	8060	Silver Wraith	WYA31	As 9173
9258	Oct. 1947	Saloon	8060	Silver Wraith	WVA77	As 9173
9259	Oct. 1947	Saloon	8060	Silver Wraith	WVA76	As 9173
9260	Mar. 1948	Saloon	8060	Silver Wraith	WYA64	As 9173
9261	Jan. 1948	Saloon	8060	Silver Wraith	WVA57	As 9173
9262	Dec. 1947	Saloon	8060	Silver Wraith	WVA66	As 9173
9263	Feb. 1948	Saloon	8060	Silver Wraith	WYA8	As 9173
9264	Aug. 1947	Touring Limousine	8034	Silver Wraith	WVA11	As 9173
9265	Sept. 1947	Touring Limousine	8034	Silver Wraith	WVA58	As 9173
9266	Sept. 1947	Touring Limousine	8034	Silver Wraith	WVA15	As 9173
9267	Apr. 1947	Touring Limousine	8034	Silver Wraith	WTA19	As 9173
9268	May 1947	Touring Limousine	8034	Silver Wraith	WTA30	As 9173
9269	Aug. 1947	Touring Limousine	8034	Silver Wraith	WTA84	As 9173
9270	June 1947	Saloon	8060	Silver Wraith	WTA11	As 9173
9271	Sept. 1947	Saloon	8060	Silver Wraith	WVA61	As 9173

BODY NO	DATE OF DELIVERY	TYPE OF BODY	DESIGN NO	CHASSIS	CHASSIS NO	REMARKS	
9272	Aug. 1947	Touring Limousine	8034	Silver Wraith	WVA18	As 9173	
9273	Aug. 1947	Touring Limousine	8034	Silver Wraith	WVA1	As 9173	
9274	Aug. 1947	Touring Limousine	8034	Silver Wraith	WVA3	As 9173	
9275	Sept. 1947	Touring Limousine	8034	Silver Wraith	WVA14	As 9173	
9276	Oct. 1947	Touring Limousine	8034	Silver Wraith	WVA16	As 9173	
9278	Oct. 1947	Sedanca de Ville	8141/52	Silver Wraith	WTA62	Special front	
9280	Oct. 1946	Touring Limousine	8098	Silver Wraith		Teviot I	Jig Body
9281	Sept. 1947	Touring Limousine	8098	Silver Wraith	WVA38	As 9280	Jig Body
9282		Touring Limousine	8098	Silver Wraith		As 9280	
9283	Feb. 1948	Touring Limousine	8098	Silver Wraith	WYA80	As 9280	
9284	Mar. 1948	Touring Limousine	8098	Silver Wraith	WVA67	As 9280	
9285	Mar. 1948	Touring Limousine	8098	Silver Wraith	WZB5	As 9280	
9286	Apr. 1948	Touring Limousine	8098	Silver Wraith	WZB7	As 9280	
9287	Mar. 1948	Touring Limousine	8098	Silver Wraith	WZB9	As 9280	
9288	Apr. 1948	Touring Limousine	8098	Silver Wraith	WZB10	As 9280	
9289	June 1948	Saloon	8122	Silver Wraith	WZB24	As 9280	
9290	Mar. 1948	Saloon	8122	Silver Wraith	WZB33	As 9280	
9291	June 1948	Touring Limousine	8098	Silver Wraith	WZB38	As 9280	
9292	May 1948	Touring Limousine	8098	Silver Wraith	WZB39	As 9280	
9293	July 1948	Touring Limousine	8098	Silver Wraith	WZB43	As 9280	
9294	May 1948	Touring Limousine	8098	Silver Wraith	WZB44	As 9280	
9295	July 1948	Touring Limousine	8098	Silver Wraith	WZB45	As 9280	
9296	June 1948	Touring Limousine	8098	Silver Wraith	WZB49	As 9280	
9297	Oct. 1948	Touring Limousine	8098	Silver Wraith	WZB50	As 9280	
9298	May 1948	Touring Limousine	8098	Silver Wraith	WZB51	As 9280	
9299	July 1948	Touring Limousine	8098	Silver Wraith	WZB62	As 9280	
9300	May 1948	Touring Limousine	8098	Silver Wraith	WZB64	As 9280	
9301	July 1948	Touring Limousine	8098	Silver Wraith	WAB1	As 9280	
9302	Oct. 1948	Touring Limousine	8098	Silver Wraith	WAB4	As 9280	
9303	July 1948	Touring Limousine	8098	Silver Wraith	WZB65	As 9280	
9304	Sept. 1948	Touring Limousine	8098	Silver Wraith	WAB5	As 9280	
9305	July 1948	Touring Limousine	8098	Silver Wraith	WAB6	As 9280	
9306	Aug. 1948	Touring Limousine	8098	Silver Wraith	WAB18	As 9280	
9307	July 1948	Touring Limousine	8098	Silver Wraith	WAB7	As 9280	
9308	July 1948	Touring Limousine	8098	Silver Wraith	WAB22	As 9280	
9309	July 1948	Touring Limousine	8098	Silver Wraith	WAB24	As 9280	
9310	July 1948	Touring Limousine	8098	Silver Wraith	WAB25	As 9280	
9311	Aug. 1948	Touring Limousine	8098	Silver Wraith	WAB29	As 9280	
9312	Aug. 1948	Touring Limousine	8098	Silver Wraith	WAB33	As 9280	
9313	Aug. 1948	Touring Limousine	8098	Silver Wraith	WAB33	As 9280	
9314	Sept. 1948	Touring Limousine	8098	Silver Wraith	WAB14	As 9280	
9315	July 1948	Touring Limousine	8098	Silver Wraith	WAB40	As 9280	
9316	Aug. 1948	Touring Limousine	8098	Silver Wraith	WAB39	As 9280	
9317	Aug. 1948	Touring Limousine	8098	Silver Wraith	WAB28	As 9280	
9318	Jan. 1949	Touring Limousine	8098	Silver Wraith	WAB41	As 9280	
9319	Aug. 1948	Touring Limousine	8098	Silver Wraith	WAB50	As 9280	
9320	Aug. 1948	Touring Limousine	8098	Silver Wraith	WAB48	As 9280	
9321	Sept. 1948	Touring Limousine	8098	Silver Wraith	WAB47	As 9280	
9322	Aug. 1948	Saloon	8122	Silver Wraith	WAB21	As 9280	

BODY NO	DATE OF DELIVERY	TYPE OF BODY	DESIGN NO	CHASSIS	CHASSIS NO	REMARKS
9323	Aug. 1948	Touring Limousine	8098	Silver Wraith	WAB49	As 9280
9324	Oct. 1948	Touring Limousine	8098	Silver Wraith	WAB59	As 9280
9325	Nov. 1948	Touring Limousine	8098	Silver Wraith	WAB57	As 9280
9326	Sept. 1948	Touring Limousine	8098	Silver Wraith	WAB62	As 9280
9327	Aug. 1948	Touring Limousine	8098	Silver Wraith	WCB3	As 9280
9328	Sept. 1948	Touring Limousine	8098	Silver Wraith	WAB58	As 9280
9329	Sept. 1948	Touring Limousine	8098	Silver Wraith	WCB8	As 9280
9330	July 1949	Coupé Cabriolet	8090	Silver Wraith	WDC31	As 9280
9343	Apr. 1947	Limousine	8134	Silver Wraith	WYA45	As 9256
9347	Nov. 1947	Limousine	8125	Silver Wraith	WVA54	As 9256
9355	Nov. 1948	Saloon	8181	Silver Wraith	WCB57	Earl's Court Show 1948
9360	Aug. 1948	Touring Limousine	8098	Silver Wraith	WCB2	
9361	Dec. 1948	Touring Limousine	8098	Silver Wraith	WCB37	Fixed roof
9362	Sept. 1948	Touring Limousine	8098	Silver Wraith	WCB1	
9389	Oct. 1947	Touring Limousine	8034	Silver Wraith	WVA33	As 9173
9390	Nov. 1947	Touring Limousine	8034	Silver Wraith	WVA27	As 9173
9391	Oct. 1947	Touring Limousine	8034	Silver Wraith	WVA39	As 9173
9392	Oct. 1947	Touring Limousine	8034	Silver Wraith	WVA17	As 9173
9393	Oct. 1947	Touring Limousine	8034	Silver Wraith	WVA31	As 9173
9394	Dec. 1947	Touring Limousine	8034	Silver Wraith	WVA40	As 9173
9395	Jan. 1948	Touring Limousine	8034	Silver Wraith	WVA32	As 9173
9396	May 1948	Touring Limousine	8034	Silver Wraith	WYA58	As 9173
9397	Feb. 1948	Saloon	8060	Silver Wraith	WYA70	As 9173
9398	May 1948	Saloon	8060	Silver Wraith	WZB17	As 9173
9399	Feb. 1948	Touring Limousine	8034	Silver Wraith	WVA56	As 9173
9400	Dec. 1947	Touring Limousine	8034	Silver Wraith	WVA50	As 9173
9401	Feb. 1948	Touring Limousine	8034	Silver Wraith	WVA10	As 9173
9402	Nov. 1947	Touring Limousine	8034	Silver Wraith	WYA10	As 9173
9403	Dec. 1947	Touring Limousine	8034	Silver Wraith	WVA51	As 9173
9404	Nov. 1947	Touring Limousine	8034	Silver Wraith	WVA55	As 9173
9405	Jan. 1948	Touring Limousine	8034	Silver Wraith	WVA55	As 9173
9406	Dec. 1947	Touring Limousine	8034	Silver Wraith	WVA64	As 9173
9407	Jan. 1948	Touring Limousine	8034	Silver Wraith	WYA27	As 9173
9408	Jan .1948	Touring Limousine	8034	Silver Wraith	WVA68	As 9173
9409	Dec. 1947	Touring Limousine	8034	Silver Wraith	WVA78	As 9173
9410	Feb. 1947	Touring Limousine	8034	Silver Wraith	WVA65	As 9173
9411	Mar. 1948	Touring Limousine	8034	Silver Wraith	WYA34	As 9173
9412	Mar. 1948	Touring Limousine	8034	Silver Wraith	WYA39	As 9173
9413	Feb. 1948	Touring Limousine	8034	Silver Wraith	WYA44	As 9173
9414	Mar. 1948	Touring Limousine	8034	Silver Wraith	WYA50	As 9173
9415	June 1948	Touring Limousine	8034	Silver Wraith	WYA56	As 9173
9416	Mar. 1948	Touring Limousine	8034	Silver Wraith	WYA57	As 9173
9417	Mar. 1948	Touring Limousine	8034	Silver Wraith	WZB33	As 9173
9418	June 1948	Touring Limousine	8034	Silver Wraith	WZB34	As 9173
9419	Feb. 1948	Limousine	8134	Silver Wraith	WYA63	
9422	May 1948	Limousine	8134	Silver Wraith	WYA51	
9423	May 1948	Limousine	8134	Silver Wraith	WYA71	As 9343
9435	Jan. 1949	Coupé Cabriolet	8090	Silver Wraith	WCB6	
9438	Oct. 1948	Touring Limousine	8098	Silver Wraith	WCB24	As 9280

HOOPER

BODY NO	DATE OF DELIVERY	TYPE OF BODY	DESIGN NO	CHASSIS	CHASSIS NO	REMARKS
9439	Sept. 1948	Touring Limousine	8098	Silver Wraith	WCB23	As 9280 E.C. Show 1948
9440	Sept. 1948	Touring Limousine	8098	Silver Wraith	WCB29	As 9280
9441	Dec. 1948	Touring Limousine	8098	Silver Wraith	WCB42	As 9280
9442	Jan. 1949	Touring Limousine	8098	Silver Wraith	WCR16	As 9280
9443	Dec. 1948	Touring Limousine	8098	Silver Wraith	WCB52	As 9280
9444	Dec. 1948	Touring Limousine	8098	Silver Wraith	WCB53	As 9280
9445	Dec. 1948	Touring Limousine	8098	Silver Wraith	WCB49	As 9280
9446	Dec. 1948	Touring Limousine	8098	Silver Wraith	WCB65	As 9280
9447	Dec. 1948	Touring Limousine	8098	Silver Wraith	WCB68	As 9280
9448	Dec. 1948	Touring Limousine	8098	Silver Wraith	WDC6	As 9280
9449	Jan. 1949	Touring Limousine	8098	Silver Wraith	WCB73	As 9280
9450	Jan. 1949	Touring Limousine	8098	Silver Wraith	WCB60	As 9280
9451	Jan. 1949	Touring Limousine	8098	Silver Wraith	WCB71	As 9280
9452	Jan. 1949	Touring Limousine	8098	Silver Wraith	WDC5	As 9280
9453	Jan. 1949	Touring Limousine	8098	Silver Wraith	WDC76	New York Show 1949
9454	Apr. 1949	Touring Limousine	8098	Silver Wraith	WDC25	As 9280
9455	Feb. 1949	Touring Limousine	8098	Silver Wraith	WDC40	As 9280
9456	Feb. 1949	Touring Limousine	8098	Silver Wraith	WDC21	As 9280
9457	Feb. 1949	Touring Limousine	8098	Silver Wraith	WDC45	As 9280
9458	Mar. 1949	Saloon	8122	Silver Wraith	WDC53	As 9280
9459	Jan. 1949	Saloon	8122	Silver Wraith	WCB36	As 9280
9460	Feb. 1949	Saloon	8122	Silver Wraith	WDC55	As 9280
9461	Mar. 1949	Saloon	8122	Silver Wraith	WDC56	As 9280
9462	Jan. 1949	Touring Limousine	8193	Silver Wraith	WDC9	As 9280
9466	Dec. 1948	Touring Limousine	8034A	Silver Wraith	WCB54	As 9173
9467	Feb. 1949	Touring Limousine	8034A	Silver Wraith	WDC2	As 9173
9468	Feb. 1949	Touring Limousine	8034A	Silver Wraith	WDC24	As 9173
9469	Jan. 1949	Saloon	8060A	Silver Wraith	WDC1	As 9173
9470	Jan. 1949	Saloon	8060A	Silver Wraith	WCB61	As 9173
9474	Jan. 1949	Touring Limousine	8098	Silver Wraith	WDC37	As 9280
9475	Feb. 1949	Touring Limousine	8098	Silver Wraith	WDC48	As 9280
9476	Feb. 1949	Touring Limousine	8098	Silver Wraith	WDC14	As 9280
9477	Feb. 1949	Touring Limousine	8098	Silver Wraith	WDC42	As 9280
9478	Feb. 1949	Touring Limousine	8098	Silver Wraith	WDC58	As 9280
9479	Mar. 1949	Touring Limousine	8098	Silver Wraith	WDC61	As 9280
9480	Apr. 1949	Touring Limousine	8098	Silver Wraith	WDC50	As 9280
9481	Mar. 1949	Touring Limousine	8098	Silver Wraith	WDC75	As 9280
9482	Mar. 1949	Touring Limousine	8098	Silver Wraith	WDC72	As 9280
9483	Mar. 1949	Touring Limousine	8098	Silver Wraith	WDC73	As 9280
9484	Apr. 1949	Touring Limousine	8098	Silver Wraith	WDC84	As 9280
9485	Mar. 1949	Touring Limousine	8098	Silver Wraith	WDC92	As 9280
9486	Apr. 1949	Touring Limousine	8098	Silver Wraith	WDC99	As 9280
9487	Apr. 1949	Touring Limousine	8098	Silver Wraith	WDC98	As 9280
9488	Apr. 1949	Touring Limousine	8098	Silver Wraith	WDC85	As 9280
9489	Apr. 1949	Touring Limousine	8098	Silver Wraith	WDC91	As 9280
9490	May 1949	Touring Limousine	8098	Silver Wraith	WFC1	As 9280
9491	May 1949	Touring Limousine	8098	Silver Wraith	WFC24	As 9280
9492	June 1949	Touring Limousine	8098	Silver Wraith	WFC30	As 9280
9493	May 1949	Touring Limousine	8098	Silver Wraith	WFC9	As 9280

BODY NO	DATE OF DELIVERY	TYPE OF BODY	DESIGN NO	CHASSIS	CHASSIS NO	REMARKS
9505	June 1949	Saloon	8181	Silver Wraith	WDC12	As 9355
9506	Dec. 1949	Saloon	8181	Silver Wraith	WGC31	As 9355
9507	Apr. 1949	Saloon	8181	Silver Wraith	WFC15	As 9355
9508	Dec. 1949	Touring Limousine	8181	Silver Wraith	WFC18	As 9355
9509	Apr. 1949	Saloon	8181	Silver Wraith	WDC93	As 9355
9510	Feb. 1950	Touring Limousine	8235	Silver Wraith	WGC81	As 9570
9511	Apr. 1950	Saloon	8181	Silver Wraith	WGC52	As 9355
9512	Mar. 1950	Touring Limousine	8235	Silver Wraith	WGC84	As 9570
9513	Mar. 1949	Touring Limousine	8193	Silver Wraith	WDC67	Teviot with concealed running boards
9514	Apr. 1949	Limousine	8195	Silver Wraith	WFC22	As 9570
9516	June 1949	Touring Limousine	8098	Silver Wraith	WFC38	As 9280
9517	June 1949	Touring Limousine	8098	Silver Wraith	WFC27	As 9280
9518	July 1949	Touring Limousine	8098	Silver Wraith	WFC53	As 9280
9519	July 1949	Touring Limousine	8098	Silver Wraith	WFC64	As 9280
9520	Aug. 1949	Touring Limousine	8098	Silver Wraith	WFC44	As 9280
9521	Aug. 1949	Touring Limousine	8098	Silver Wraith	WFC47	As 9280
9522	July 1949	Touring Limousine	8098	Silver Wraith	WFC70	As 9280
9523	June 1949	Touring Limousine	8098	Silver Wraith	WFC27	As 9280
9524	Aug. 1949	Touring Limousine	8098	Silver Wraith	WFC79	As 9280
9525	Sept. 1949	Touring Limousine	8098	Silver Wraith	WFC67	As 9280
9526	Aug. 1949	Touring Limousine	8098	Silver Wraith	WFC77	As 9280
9527	Aug. 1949	Touring Limousine	8098	Silver Wraith	WFC85	As 9280
9528	Sept. 1949	Touring Limousine	8098	Silver Wraith	WFC88	As 9280
9529	Sept 1949	Touring Limousine	8098	Silver Wraith	WFC92	As 9280
9530	Aug. 1949	Touring Limousine	8098	Silver Wraith	WFC98	As 9280
9531	Oct. 1949	Touring Limousine	8098	Silver Wraith	WGC7	As 9280
9532	Oct. 1949	Touring Limousine	8098	Silver Wraith	WGC24	As 9280
9533	Apr. 1949	Saloon	8122	Silver Wraith	WDC77	As 9280
9534	Apr. 1949	Saloon	8122	Silver Wraith	WFC11	As 9280
9535	Aug. 1949	Saloon	8122	Silver Wraith	WFC34	As 9280
9536	Mar. 1949	Limousine	8195	Silver Wraith	WDC64	As 9343 'H' seats
9543	Dec. 1949	Touring Limousine	8098	Silver Wraith	WGC35	As 9280
9544	July 1949	Touring Limousine	8098	Silver Wraith	WFC59	As 9280
9545	Oct. 1949	Touring Limousine	8098	Silver Wraith	WFC20	As 9280
9546	Aug. 1949	Touring Limousine	8098	Silver Wraith	WFC39	As 9280
9547	Sept. 1949	Touring Limousine	8098	Silver Wraith	WFC35	As 9280
9548	Dec. 1949	Touring Limousine	8098	Silver Wraith	WGC39	As 9280
9549	Jan. 1950	Touring Limousine	8098	Silver Wraith	WGC42	As 9280
9550	Jan. 1950	Touring Limousine	8098	Silver Wraith	LWGC70	As 9280
9551	Jan. 1950	Touring Limousine	8098	Silver Wraith	WGC44	As 9280
9552	Jan. 1950	Touring Limousine	8098	Silver Wraith	WGC57	As 9280
9561	Sept. 1949	Landaulette	8178	Silver Wraith	WBC1	'H' pattern seats
9562	Oct. 1949	Limousine	8195	Silver Wraith	WGC12	
9567	Nov. 1949	Limousine	8195	Silver Wraith	WGC4	As 9562 'H' seats
9568	Sept. 1949	Saloon	8234	Silver Wraith	WGC16	Hooper Stand Earl's Court 1948
9570	Sept. 1949	Touring Limousine	8235	Silver Wraith	WGC18	Teviot II
9572	Apr. 1950	Touring Limousine	8235	Silver Wraith	WGC87	As 9570
9573	May 1950	Touring Limousine	8235	Silver Wraith	WGC85	As 9570

BODY NO	DATE OF DELIVERY	TYPE OF BODY	DESIGN NO	CHASSIS	CHASSIS NO	REMARKS
9574	Apr. 1950	Touring Limousine	8235	Silver Wraith	WGC93	As 9570
9575	Jan. 1950	Limousine	8195	Silver Wraith	WGC74	As 9567 Copenhagen Show
9576	July 1950	Limousine	8195	Silver Wraith	WHD58	As 9567
9577	May 1950	Limousine	8195	Silver Wraith	WHD9	As 9567
9593	May 1950	7 Seater Limousine	8255	Silver Wraith	LWGC88	As 9567
9607	June 1950	Touring Limousine	8235	Silver Wraith	WHD19	As 9571
9608	Apr. 1950	Touring Limousine	8235	Silver Wraith	WHD7	Glass roof panel
9609	June 1950	Touring Limousine	8235	Silver Wraith	WHD28	As 9570
9610	Aug. 1950	Touring Limousine	8235	Silver Wraith	LWHD62	S/S roof
9611	July 1950	Touring Limousine	8235	Silver Wraith	WHD59	
9623	Dec. 1950	Touring Limousine	8283	Silver Wraith	WHD91	Teviot III R.R. Stand EC 1950
9624	Feb. 1951	Touring Limousine	8283	Silver Wraith	WLE14	As 9623
9625	June 1951	Touring Limousine	8283	Silver Wraith	WLE19	As 9623
9626	June 1951	Touring Limousine	8283	Silver Wraith	WME5	As 9623
9627	June 1951	Touring Limousine	8283	Silver Wraith	WME29	As 9623
9628	Aug. 1951	Saloon	8303	Silver Wraith	WME38	As 9623 S/S roof
9629	Jan. 1951	Saloon	8303	Silver Wraith	WHD83	Teviot III Hooper Stand EC 1950
9630	July 1951	Touring Limousine	8283	Silver Wraith	WME14	As 9623
9631	Aug. 1951	Saloon	8303	Silver Wraith	WME43	As 9623
9632	Oct. 1951	Touring Limousine	8283	Silver Wraith	WME75	As 9623
9633	Dec. 1951	Touring Limousine	8283	Silver Wraith	WOF18	As 9623
9634	Jan. 1952	Touring Limousine	8283	Silver Wraith	WOF52	As 9623
9643	Sept. 1950	Saloon	8122	Silver Wraith	LWHD95	
9644	Sept. 1951	Touring Limousine	8283	Silver Wraith	WME55	As 9623
9645	Dec. 1951	Touring Limousine	8283	Silver Wraith	WOF12	As 9623 R.R. Stand EC 1951
9646	Aug. 1951	Saloon	8303	Silver Wraith	WME80	As 9623
9647	May 1951	Touring Limousine	8283	Silver Wraith	WLE26	As 9623
9648	Feb. 1952	Touring Limousine	8283	Silver Wraith	WOF6	As 9623
9649	Nov. 1951	Touring Limousine	8283	Silver Wraith	WOF24	As 9623
9650	Dec. 1951	Saloon	8303	Silver Wraith	WOF31	As 9623
9651	Dec. 1951	Touring Limousine	8283	Silver Wraith	WOF17	As 9623
9652	Mar. 1952	Touring Limousine	8283	Silver Wraith	WOF72	As 9623
9653	Jan. 1952	Touring Limousine	8283	Silver Wraith	WOF44	As 9623
9654	Mar. 1952	Touring Limousine	8283	Silver Wraith	WOF59	As 9623
9655	Mar. 1952	Touring Limousine	8283	Silver Wraith	WSG5	As 9623
9656	Apr. 1952	Touring Limousine	8283	Silver Wraith	WSG10	As 9623
9657	July 1952	Touring Limousine	8283	Silver Wraith	WSG20	As 9623
9658	Apr. 1952	Saloon	8303	Silver Wraith	WOF76	As 9623
9659	Feb. 1952	Saloon	8303	Silver Wraith	WOF56	As 9623
9660	June 1952	Touring Limousine	8283	Silver Wraith	WSG38	As 9623
9661	May 1952	Saloon	8317	Silver Wraith	WSG17	As 9623 4 Light
9663	Sept. 1951	Limousine	8292	Phantom IV	4AF10	1st Phantom IV
9689	Mar. 1951	7 Seater Limousine	8195	Silver Wraith	WME19	As 9562
9690	June 1951	7 Seater Limousine	8195	Silver Wraith	WME67	As 9562
9691	July 1951	7 Seater Limousine	8195	Silver Wraith	WME82	As 9562
9692	Oct. 1951	7 Seater Limousine	8195	Silver Wraith	WME85	As 9562
9719	July 1951	Limousine	8307	Phantom IV	4AF12	
9726	Apr. 1952	Touring Limousine	8283	Silver Wraith	LWSG7	As 9623
9727	July 1952	Touring Limousine	8283	Silver Wraith	WSG22	As 9623

BODY NO	DATE OF DELIVERY	TYPE OF BODY	DESIGN NO	CHASSIS	CHASSIS NO	REMARKS
9728	Aug. 1952	Touring Limousine	8283	Silver Wraith	WSG57	As 9623
9729	Oct. 1952	Touring Limousine	8283	Silver Wraith	WVH11	As 9623
9730	Oct. 1952	Touring Limousine	8283	Silver Wraith	WSG65	As 9623
9731	Oct. 1952	Touring Limousine	8283	Silver Wraith	WVH12	As 9623
9732	Sept. 1952	Touring Limousine	8283	Silver Wraith	WVH16	As 9623 Paris Salon 1952
9733	Oct. 1952	Saloon	8303	Silver Wraith	WSG36	As 9623
9734	Dec. 1952	Touring Limousine	8283	Silver Wraith	WVH18	As 9623
9735	Jan. 1953	Touring Limousine	8283	Silver Wraith	WVH 33	As 9623
9736	Oct. 1952	Touring Limousine	8283	Silver Wraith	LWVH15	As 9623
9737	Jan. 1953	Saloon	8303	Silver Wraith	LWVH28	As 9623
9738	Dec. 1952	Touring Limousine	8283	Silver Wraith	WVH39	As 9623
9739	Apr. 1953	Touring Limousine	8283	Silver Wraith	LWVH82	As 9623
9740	Dec. 1952	Touring Limousine	8283	Silver Wraith	WVH9	As 9623 R.R. Stand EC 1592
9741	Dec. 1952	Touring Limousine	8283	Silver Wraith	WVH32	As 9623
9742	Jan. 1953	Touring Limousine	8283	Silver Wraith	WVH35	As 9623
9743	Jan. 1953	Touring Limousine	8283	Silver Wraith	WVH52	As 9623
9744	Apr. 1953	Touring Limousine	8283	Silver Wraith	WVH62	As 9623
9745	Apr. 1953	Touring Limousine	8283	Silver Wraith	WVH51	As 9623
9746	June 1953	7 Seater Limousine	8330	Silver Wraith	ALW49	$\frac{1}{4}$ windows as Teviot
9747	Oct. 1952	7 Seater Limousine	8330	Silver Wraith	ALW23	
9748	Nov. 1952	7 Seater Limousine	8330	Silver Wraith	ALW37	R.R. Stand Earl's Court 1952
9749	July 1953	Limousine	8381	Silver Wraith	BLW15	
9750	May 1952	Sedanca de Ville	8293	Phantom IV	4AF20	
9813	Apr. 1953	Touring Limousine	8283	Silver Wraith	WSG63	As 9623
9814	May 1953	Touring Limousine	8283	Silver Wraith	WVH71	
9815	Feb. 1953	Touring Limousine	8283	Silver Wraith	LWVH56	
9816	Mar. 1953	Touring Limousine	8283	Silver Wraith	WVH43	
9817	Mar. 1953	Touring Limousine	8283	Silver Wraith	WVH63	
9818	May 1953	Touring Limousine	8283	Silver Wraith	LWVH89	
9819	July 1952	Saloon	8317	Silver Wraith	WSG6	As 9862 4 Light
9820	May 1953	Touring Limousine	8283	Silver Wraith	LWVH87	
9821	May 1953	Touring Limousine	8283	Silver Wraith	WVH55	
9822	Aug. 1953	Saloon	8317	Silver Wraith	WVH102	4 Light
9823	Sept. 1953	Touring Limousine	8283	Silver Wraith	LWVH116	
9824	July 1953	Touring Limousine	8283	Silver Wraith	WVH97	
9862	Nov. 1951	Saloon	8317	Silver Wraith	WOF5	4 Light Prototype
9866	Oct. 1952	Touring Limousine	8333	Silver Wraith	ALW10	
9867	May 1952	4 Door Convertible	8335	Silver Wraith	ALW11	P.O. head Geneva Show 1953
9875	Feb. 1953	2 Door D/H Coupé	8372	Silver Wraith	WVH37	Radiator 4" forward
9889	Oct. 1953	Sedanca de Ville	8359	Silver Wraith	ALW47	
9890	Mar. 1953	Limousine	8361	Phantom IV	4BP1	
9891	Mar. 1953	Limousine	8370	Phantom IV	4BP3	
9892	Sept. 1953	D/H Coupé	8371	Silver Wraith	WVH40	
9893	Feb. 1953	4 Door D/H Coupé	8373	Silver Wraith	WVH74	Geneva Show 1953
9894	Feb. 1953	Limousine	8330	Silver Wraith	ALW40	As 9747 Geneva Show 1953
9895	May 1953	Limousine	8330	Silver Wraith	LBLW4	As 9747
9896	June 1953	Limousine	8330	Silver Wraith	BLW30	As 9747
9897	Sept. 1953	Limousine	8330	Silver Wraith	BLW19	As 9747

BODY NO	DATE OF DELIVERY	TYPE OF BODY	DESIGN NO	CHASSIS	CHASSIS NO	REMARKS
9898	May 1953	Limousine	8330	Silver Wraith	BLW17	As 9747
9899	July 1953	Limousine	8330	Silver Wraith	LBLW29	As 9747
9900	Aug. 1953	Limousine	8330	Silver Wraith	LBLW28	As 9794
9933	May 1953	Touring Limousine	8098	Silver Wraith	WVH65	As 9280 Teviot I
9936	June 1953	Touring Limousine	8390	Silver Wraith	LBLW14	All metal,
9937	July 1953	7 Seater Limousine	8330	Silver Wraith	LBLW25	As 9747
9938	Aug. 1953	7 Seater Limousine	8330	Silver Wraith	LBLW31	As 9747
9939	Aug. 1953	7 Seater Limousine	8330	Silver Wraith	LBLW33	As 9747
9940	Sept. 1953	7 Seater Limousine	8330	Silver Wraith	BLW22	As 9747
9941	May 1954	Landaulette	8399	Phantom IV	4BP5	
9944	Sept. 1953	7 Seater Limousine	8330	Silver Wraith	BLW67	As 9747 Paris Salon 1953
9945	Apr. 1954	7 Seater Limousine	8330	Silver Wraith	CLW1	As 9747
9946	Feb. 1954	7 Seater Limousine	8330	Silver Wraith	BLW75	As 9747
9947	Nov. 1953	7 Seater Limousine	8330	Silver Wraith	BLW47	As 9747 R.R. Stand EC 1953
9948	Dec. 1954	7 Seater Limousine	8330	Silver Wraith	DLW71	As 9747
9949	Jan. 1954	7 Seater Limousine	8330	Silver Wraith	LBLW74	As 9747
9954	Nov. 1953	Touring Limousine	8390	Silver Wraith	BLW66	As 9936
9955	Dec. 1953	Touring Limousine	8390	Silver Wraith	LBLW57	As 9936
9956	Nov. 1953	Touring Limousine	8390	Silver Wraith	BLW50	As 9936 Scottish Show 1953
9957	Dec. 1953	Touring Limousine	8390	Silver Wraith	BLW62	As 9936
9958	Nov. 1953	Touring Limousine	8390	Silver Wraith	BLW69	As 9936 Scottish Show 1953
9959	Dec. 1954	Touring Limousine	8390	Silver Wraith	DLW66	As 9936
9960	Mar. 1954	Touring Limousine	8390	Silver Wraith	BLW95	As 9936
9961	Apr. 1954	Saloon	8409	Silver Wraith	CLW2	As 9936
9962	Apr. 1954	Saloon	8409	Silver Wraith	CLW6	As 9936
9963	Apr. 1954	Touring Limousine	8390	Silver Wraith	BLW94	As 9936
9964	Apr. 1954	Touring Limousine	8390	Silver Wraith	BLW98	As 9936
9965	June 1954	Touring Limousine	8390	Silver Wraith	CLW25	As 9936
9974	Apr. 1954	Saloon	8401	Silver Dawn	SNF105	As 9622
9975	June 1954	7 Seater Limousine	8400	Silver Wraith	CLW22	As 9747
9976	Sept. 1956	7 Seater Limousine	8400	Silver Wraith	FLW6	As 9747
9977	Mar. 1955	7 Seater Limousine	8400	Silver Wraith	DLW92	As 9747
9978	May 1954	7 Seater Limousine	8400	Silver Wraith	BLW97	As 9747
9979		7 Seater Limousine	8400	Silver Wraith	DLW47	As 9747 R.R. Stand EC 1954
9980	Apr. 1955	7 Seater Limousine	8400	Silver Wraith	DLW78	As 9747
9981	May 1955	7 Seater Limousine	8400	Silver Wraith	DLW88	As 9747
9982	Aug. 1956	7 Seater Limousine	8400	Silver Wraith	ELW98	As 9747
9983	Jan. 1956	7 Seater Limousine	8400	Silver Wraith	ELW34	As 9747
9984	Nov. 1955	7 Seater Limousine	8400	Silver Wraith	LELW16	As 9747
9985	Nov. 1955	7 Seater Limousine	8400	Silver Wraith	ELW11	As 9747 R.R. Stand EC 1955
9986	July 1954	7 Seater Limousine	8400	Silver Wraith	DLW17	As 9747
9987	Jan. 1956	7 Seater Limousine	8400	Silver Wraith	ELW29	As 9747
9988	Apr. 1956	7 Seater Limousine	8400	Silver Wraith	ELW66	As 9747
9989	July 1956	7 Seater Limousine	8460	Silver Wraith	ELW89	As 9747 Built-in headlamps
9990	June 1954	Touring Limousine	8390	Silver Wraith	CLW33	As 9936
9991	Sept. 1954	Touring Limousine	8390	Silver Wraith	DLW34	As 9936
9992	June 1954	Touring Limousine	8390	Silver Wraith	CLW15	As 9936
9993	Nov. 1954	Touring Limousine	8390	Silver Wraith	LDLW60	As 9936

BODY NO	DATE OF DELIVERY	TYPE OF BODY	DESIGN NO	CHASSIS	CHASSIS NO	REMARKS
9994	Jan. 1955	Touring Limousine	8390	Silver Wraith	DLW85	As 9936
9995	Nov. 1954	Touring Limousine	8390	Silver Wraith	DLW56	As 9936
9996	Feb. 1954	Touring Limousine	8390	Silver Wraith	DLW87	As 9936
9997	May 1955	Touring Limousine	8390	Silver Wraith	DLW89	As 9936
9998	Nov. 1954	Touring Limousine	8390	Silver Wraith	LDLW18	As 9936	4 Light
9999	July 1954	Touring Limousine	8390	Silver Wraith	DLW3	As 9936	4 Light
10000	July 1954	Touring Limousine	8390	Silver Wraith	CLW35	As 9936	4 Light
10001	Nov. 1954	Touring Limousine	8390	Silver Wraith	DLW68	As 9936	4 Light
10002	Oct. 1954	Touring Limousine	8390	Silver Wraith	DLW25	As 9936	4 Light
10003	Oct. 1954	Touring Limousine	8390	Silver Wraith	DLW32	As 9936	4 Light
10004	Oct. 1954	Touring Limousine	8390	Silver Wraith	DLW16	As 9936	4 Light
10005	Nov. 1954	Touring Limousine	8390	Silver Wraith	DLW55	As 9936	4 Light EC 1954
10006	Oct. 1954	Saloon	8409	Silver Wraith	DLW37	As 9936
10007	Jan. 1955	Touring Limousine	8390	Silver Wraith	DLW64	As 9936
10008	June 1954	Landaulette	8403	Silver Wraith	BLW92	As 9936
10010	May 1954	Saloon	8401	Silver Dawn	SOG52	As 9622
10011	July 1954	Saloon	8401	Silver Dawn	LSOG98	As 9622
10027	Nov. 1954	Saloon	8401	Silver Dawn	SRH44	As 9622	Hooper Stand EC 1954
10028	Dec. 1954	Saloon	8401	Silver Dawn	STH99	As 9622
10029	Oct. 1954	Saloon	8401	Silver Dawn	SRH48	As 9622
10030	Nov. 1954	Saloon	8401	Silver Dawn	SRH66	As 9622
10031	Sept. 1954	Saloon	8401	Silver Dawn	SRH46	As 9622
10060	Apr. 1955	Touring Limousine	8390	Silver Wraith	DLW135	As 9936
10061	Mar. 1955	Touring Limousine	8390	Silver Wraith	DLW140	As 9936
10062	Apr. 1955	Touring Limousine	8422	Silver Wraith	DLW133	As 9936	4 Light
10063		Touring Limousine	8390	Silver Wraith	DLW151	As 9936
10064	Apr. 1955	Touring Limousine	8390	Silver Wraith	DLW106	As 9936
10065	Apr. 1955	Touring Limousine	8390	Silver Wraith	DLW114	As 9936
10066	Apr. 1955	Saloon	8409	Silver Wraith	DLW109	As 9936
10067	Mar. 1955	Saloon	8409	Silver Wraith	DLW110	As 9936
10068	Mar. 1955	Touring Limousine	8390	Silver Wraith	LDLW116	As 9936
10069	May 1955	Touring Limousine	8390	Silver Wraith	DLW159	As 9936
10070	Jan. 1955	Saloon	8401	Silver Dawn	SUJ2	As 9622
10071	Feb. 1955	Saloon	8401	Silver Dawn	STH101	As 9622
10074	Jan. 1955	Saloon	8401	Silver Dawn	STH59	As 9622
10075	Mar. 1955	Saloon	8401	Silver Dawn	SUJ4	As 9622
10082	Apr. 1955	Limousine	8420	Silver Wraith	DLW98	
10083	June 1955	Touring Limousine	8390	Silver Wraith	DLW161	As 9936
10084	June 1955	Touring Limousine	8390	Silver Wraith	DLW162	As 9936
10085	May 1955	Saloon	8409	Silver Wraith	DLW139	As 9936
10086	May 1955	Touring Limousine	8390	Silver Wraith	DLW150	As 9936
10087	June 1955	Touring Limousine	8390	Silver Wraith	DLW148	As 9936
10088	June 1955	Touring Limousine	8390	Silver Wraith	DLW155	As 9936
10089	Dec. 1955	Touring Limousine	8390	Silver Wraith	ELW50	As 9936
10090	Jan. 1956	Touring Limousine	8390	Silver Wraith	ELW41	As 9936
10091	Nov. 1955	Touring Limousine	8390	Silver Wraith	LELW6	As 9936	Hooper Stand EC 1955
10092	Dec. 1955	Touring Limousine	8390	Silver Wraith	ELW38	As 9936
10095	Oct. 1956	Touring Limousine	8390	Silver Wraith	FLW10	As 9936
10096	Feb. 1956	Touring Limousine	8390	Silver Wraith	ELW48	As 9936

HOOPER

BODY NO	DATE OF DELIVERY	TYPE OF BODY	DESIGN NO	CHASSIS	CHASSIS NO	REMARKS
10097	Feb. 1956	Touring Limousine	8390	Silver Wraith	ELW65	As 9936
10098	Nov. 1956	Touring Limousine	8390	Silver Wraith	FLW24	As 9936
10099	Apr. 1956	Touring Limousine	8390	Silver Wraith	ELW58	As 9936
10100	Mar. 1956	Touring Limousine	8390	Silver Wraith	ELW60	As 9936
10101	Feb. 1956	Saloon	8409	Silver Wraith	ELW55	As 9936
10102	Nov. 1956	Touring Limousine	8455	Silver Wraith	FLW5	As 9936	Hooper Stand EC 1956
10103	Apr. 1957	Touring Limousine	8455	Silver Wraith	FLW35	As 9936
10104	Apr. 1957	Touring Limousine	8455	Silver Wraith	ELW93	As 9936
10105	Nov. 1956	Touring Limousine	8455	Silver Wraith	LFLW23	As 9936	Refrigeration
10106	Jan. 1957	Touring Limousine	8455	Silver Wraith	FLW41	As 9936
10107	Feb. 1957	Touring Limousine	8411	Silver Wraith	ELW82	As 9936	4 Light
10108	Jan. 1957	Touring Saloon	8456	Silver Wraith	FLW57	As 9936
10109	Jan. 1957	Touring Limousine	8455	Silver Wraith	FLW30	As 9936
10110	Mar. 1957	Touring Limousine	8476	Silver Wraith	FLW42	As 9936
10111	Jun. 1957	Touring Limousine	8455	Silver Wraith	LFLW87	As 9936
10112	May 1957	Touring Limousine	8455	Silver Wraith	LFLW81	As 9936
10113	July 1957	Touring Limousine	8455	Silver Wraith	LFLW93	As 9936
10114	June 1957	Saloon	8456	Silver Wraith	LFLW69	As 9936
10126	Jan. 1956	Saloon	8435	Silver Cloud	SWA46	As 10115
10130	Jan. 1956	Saloon	8435	Silver Cloud	SWA58	As 10115
10131	Feb. 1956	Saloon	8435	Silver Cloud	SWA72	As 10115
10132	Jan. 1956	Saloon	8435	Silver Cloud	SWA44	As 10115
10134	Mar. 1956	Saloon	8435	Silver Cloud	SWA92	As 10115
10158	Apr. 1956	Saloon	8435	Silver Cloud	SWA64	As 10115
10161	June 1956	Saloon	8430	Silver Cloud	SWA98	As 10115
10165	May 1956	Saloon	8430	Silver Cloud	SWA102	As 10115
10166	May 1956	Touring Limousine	8444	Silver Cloud	SWA100	As 10115 1st Touring Limousine
10169	July 1956	Saloon	8435	Silver Cloud	SXA127	As 10115
10170	Aug. 1956	Saloon	8435	Silver Cloud	SXA43	As 10115
10171	July 1956	Saloon	8435	Silver Cloud	SYB22	As 10115
10172	Sept. 1956	Saloon	8435	Silver Cloud	SYB18	As 10115
10175	July 1956	Saloon	8449	Silver Wraith	LELW74	Perspex top. Refrigeration
10176	Apr. 1956	Landaulette	8445	Silver Wraith	ELW55	*
10177	Oct. 1956	Limousine	8425	Phantom IV	4CS6	As 9890
10178	July 1956	Limousine	8460	Silver Wraith	ELW70	As 9747*
10179	Dec. 1956	Limousine	8460	Silver Wtraih	FLW17	As 9747* R.R. Stand EC 1956
10180	Feb. 1957	Limousine	8460	Silver Wraith	FLW39	As 9747*
10181	Mar. 1958	Limousine	8460	Silver Wraith	LGLW25	As 9747*
10182	Jan. 1957	Limousine	8460	Silver Wraith	FLW34	As 9747*
10183	Apr. 1958	Limousine	8460	Silver Wraith	GLW20	As 9747*
10186	Oct. 1956	Saloon	8435	Silver Cloud	SWA45	As 10115
10187	Aug. 1956	Saloon	8435	Silver Cloud	SXA125	As 10115
10190	Dec. 1956	Saloon	8435	Silver Cloud	SZB91	As 10115
10191	Feb. 1957	Saloon	8435	Silver Cloud	SZB93	As 10115
10194	Feb. 1957	Touring Limousine	8444	Silver Cloud	SZB25	As 10115† Hooper Stand EC 1956
10195	Feb. 1957	Saloon	8435	Silver Cloud	SZB27	As 10115
10196	Sept. 1956	Saloon	8435	Silver Cloud	SXA131	As 10115
10199	Jan. 1957	Touring Limousine	8444	Silver Cloud	SZB245	As 10194

* Built-in headlamps   † Exposed headlamps

BODY NO	DATE OF DELIVERY	TYPE OF BODY	DESIGN NO	CHASSIS	CHASSIS NO	REMARKS	
10200	Dec. 1956	Saloon	8435	Silver Cloud	SBC24	As 10115	
10203	May 1957	Touring Limousine	8444	Silver Cloud	SDD148	1st cut out rear spat.	
10204	Sept. 1956	Touring Limousine	8442	Silver Wraith	LELW86	As 10082	
10209		Test Body Limousine		Phantom V			
10214	Nov. 1957	Saloon	8435	Silver Cloud	SED97	As 10115	
10219	Nov. 1957	Saloon	8506	Silver Cloud	SED251	As 10115	Cut-out type spat
10223	Nov. 1957	Saloon with division	8504	Silver Cloud	ALC5	As 10115	Hooper stand EC 1957
10224	Jan. 1958	Saloon with division	8504	Silver Cloud	ALC9	As 10115	
10225	Feb. 1958	Saloon	8523	Silver Cloud	ALC12	As 10115	
10226	May 1958	Saloon with division	8504	Silver Cloud	ALC11	As 10115	
10227	Apr. 1958	Saloon with division	8504	Silver Cloud	ALC21	As 10115	
10229	June 1958	Saloon with division	8504	Silver Cloud	ALC14	As 10115	
10230	June 1958	Saloon	8523	Silver Cloud	BLC2	As 10115	
10234	July 1957	Limousine	8508	Rolls-Royce	44EX	Prototype for PV	
10237	Oct. 1958	7 Seater Limousine	8460	Silver Wraith	HLW20		Hooper Stand EC 1958
10238	Nov. 1957	7 Seater Limousine	8460	Silver Wraith	FLW98	As 9747*	Hooper Stand EC 1957
10239	July 1957	Limousine	8460	Silver Wraith	FLW90	As 9747*	R.R. Stand EC 1957
10240	Dec. 1957	7 Seater Limousine	8460	Silver Wraith	FLW97	As 9747*	
10241	Sept. 1958	7 Seater Limousine	8460	Silver Wraith	HLW19		
10242	Dec. 1958	7 Seater Limousine	8460	Silver Wraith	HLW12		
10243	Jan. 1958	Touring Limousine	8502	Silver Wraith	LFLW92	As 9936	
10244	Dec. 1957	Touring Limousine	8500	Silver Wraith	FLW99	As 9936	Hooper Stand EC 1957
10245	May 1958	Touring Limousine	8500	Silver Wraith	GLW15	As 9936	
10246	May 1958	Touring Limousine	8500	Silver Wraith	GLW12	As 9936	
10247	Apr. 1958	Touring Limousine	8516	Silver Wraith	GLW14	As 9936	Rounded rear end
10248	Apr. 1958	Touring Limousine	8500	Silver Wraith	GLW17	As 9936	
10249	July 1958	Touring Limousine	8500	Silver Wraith	HLW6	As 9936	
10250	Oct. 1958	Touring Limousine	8500	Silver Wraith	HLW8	As 9936	
10252	Dec. 1958	Landaulette	8445	Silver Wraith	HLW35		
10253	May 1959	Limousine	8460	Silver Wraith	HLW38		
10254	Feb. 1959	Limousine	8460	Silver Wraith	HLW37		
10255		Drop-head Coupé	8530	Silver Cloud	LSGE 252	Power operated head	
10262	Oct. 1959	Limousine	8569	Phantom V	5AS19	As 10234	Hooper Stand EC 1959
10267	Oct. 1959	Saloon with division	8570	Silver Cloud II	LLCA1	As 10291	Hooper Stand EC 1959
10277	Nov. 1958	Saloon with division	8504	Silver Cloud	BLC31	As 10115	Hooper Stand EC 1958
10278	Nov. 1958	Saloon with division	8504	Silver Cloud	BLC32	As 10115	
10281	May 1959	Saloon with division	8504	Silver Cloud	BLC39	As 10115	
10282	Mar. 1959	Saloon with division	8504	Silver Cloud	LCLC5	As 10115	New York Show 1959
10283	Apr. 1959	2 Door Saloon	8546	Silver Cloud	BLC35	Invalid Seat	
10284	Aug. 1959	Limousine	8460	Silver Wraith	HLW40	As 9747	
10285	Jul. 1959	Limousine	8460	Silver Wraith	HLW41	As 9747	
10286	May 1959	Saloon	8523	Silver Cloud	LCLC1	As 10115	
10287	Mar. 1959	All weather	8537	Silver Wraith	LHLW44	Removable perspex top	
10288	Apr. 1959	All weather	8548	Silver Wraith	HLW47		
10289	Apr. 1959	All weather	8548	Silver Wraith	HLW49	As 10288	
10290	Apr. 1959	All weather	8548	Silver Wraith	LHLW51	As 10288	

* Built-in headlamps

Hoopers first post war design (irreverently christened 'The Squatting Hen') a touring Limousine on a Silver Wraith chassis, design No. 8034, and possibly the first body of that design, note the number plate RR 1946. Below: another very early design No. 8034, the divided bonnet side denotes it's early date. Registration No. HTU 952.

By August 1947 the divided bonnet side had disappeared, another of design No. 8034, this time body No. 9272 on Silver Wraith, WVA 18.

The second post war body, a Sedanca de Ville version of design No. 8034. This is body No. 9174, design No. 8057 on Silver Wraith, WTA 71, although ordered in 1946 it was not delivered until December 1947.

This Limousine, body No. 9256, design No. 8056 on Silver Wraith, WTA 14, was supplied to H.R.H. the Princess Royal in December 1946.

Below: a slightly later car, body No. 9423, design No. 8134, a Limousine on Silver Wraith, WYA 71.

The High Commissioner of India's Limousine on Silver Wraith, WDC 64, body No. 9536, design No. 8195.

Built for the Copenhagen Show, the limousine pictured below is body No. 9575, design No. 8195, on Silver Wraith, WGC 74. 4 different Limousines, 3 different designs, but all very similar.

HOOPER

A Saloon, body No. 9257, design No. 8060 on Silver Wraith, WYA 31, from which the design below stems. This was the very popular Teviot, design No. 8098, a Touring Limousine, this body is No. 9476, on Silver Wraith, WDC 14. The main external difference is the exposing of the running boards which on previous designs had been covered by the outsweep of the body.

Another Teviot, Touring Limousine, design No. 8098, prepared for exhibition in America.

A Saloon version of Teviot, body No. 9460, design No. 8122, on Silver Wraith, WDC 55.

Rear interior of Teviot.

Front interior of Teviot.

Hood down and hood up views of what is termed a Coupé Cabriolet, design No. 8090, two of which were completed in January and July 1949.

Mr. Nubar Gulbenkian first Post-war Hooper bodied Rolls-Royce, a Sedanca de Ville, body No. 9278, design No. 8141/8152 on Silver Wraith, WVA 16.

H.H. The Maharajah of Mysore's Saloon, body No. 9506, design No. 8181, on Silver Wraith, WEC 31.

Below: A Landaulette for the President of Eire, body No. 9561, design No. 8178 on Silver Wraith, WEC 1, delivered in September 1949.

Earls Court Show car of 1949. Body No. 9568, a Saloon, design No. 8234 on Silver Wraith, WGC 16. Below are two Teviot II's, design No. 8235, Touring Limousines. This was a short lived design and was rapidly superceded by Teviot III. The centre car is body No. 9608 on Silver Wraith, WHD 7, at present owned by A. R. Walsh Esq.

Another Teviot II above, with below two Teviot III's, design No. 8283, Touring Limousines.

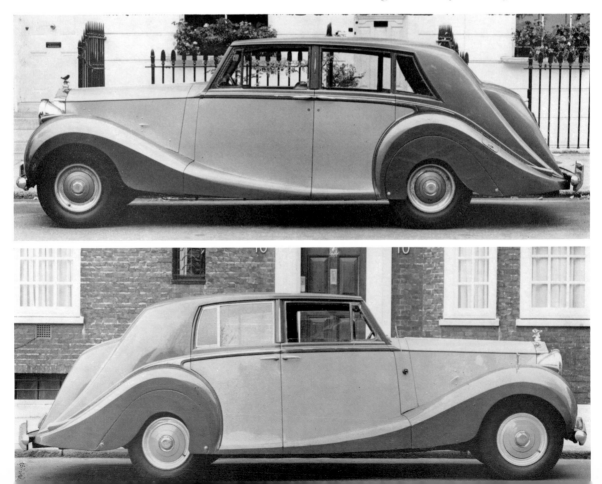

*The two lower cars on the opposite page are, in the centre, body No. 9821 on Silver Wraith,
WVH 55, and below, on WVH 63, is body No. 9817 and surprisingly, as it is a four
light body, still a design No. 8283.*

*The car illustrated on this page is the 1951 Hooper stand show car, body No. 9645, design
No. 8283 on Silver Wraith, WOF 12, a Touring Limousine.*

Phantom IV, 4AF 20, with Sedanca de Ville, body No. 9750, design No. 8293, supplied to H.H. the Aga Khan in May 1952. It is now in the United States and owned by Thomas Barratt Esq. The reproduction in black and white of a colour photograph is disappointing and does not show the rich red leather off to best effect.

Limousine, body No. 9890, design No. 8361 on Phantom IV, 4BP1, supplied to the late King Faisal of Iraq in March 1953.

Below: a 7 passenger Limousine built for the Shah of Persia on Phantom IV, 4CS6, body No. 10177, design No. 8425.

The Duke of Gloucester's Phantom IV, 4 AF10, mounted with a 7 passenger Limousine, body No. 9663, design No. 8292, and below built for the late Prince Regent of Iraq in March 1953, a Limousine, body No. 9891, design No. 8370, on Phantom IV, 4BP3. Present owner W. Davis Esq.

Her Majesty Queen Elizabeth II's Hooper Landaulette 'Jubilee', body No. 9941, design No. 8399 on Phantom IV, 4BP5.

A Landaulette supplied to the Governor of Nigeria in April 1956 is pictured below with the centre photograph showing the headlamp treatment. Body No. 10176, design No. 8445, on a long wheelbase Silver Wraith, ELW 55.

Body No. 9898, design No. 8330, a Limousine on Silver Wraith, BLW 17, and in the small centre photograph is the 1953 Earls Court Show Hooper Limousine exhibited on the Rolls-Royce stand. This car is body No. 9947, design No. 8330, on Silver Wraith, BLW 47.

The lower photograph again illustrates design No. 8330. This car, supplied to Princess Faisal of Iraq in January 1954, is body No. 9949, on Silver Wraith, LBLW 74.

Design No. 8460, two views of which are shown, was exhibited on the Rolls-Royce stand at Earls Court in 1957. It was the last Limousine design by Hoopers mounted on the Silver Wraith chassis. This car is body No. 10240 and chassis No. FLW 97.

The lower photograph shows the unusual cut away design on the floor to allow a large step on the running board for the rear passengers.

Overleaf, Limousine, body No. 10239, design No. 8460 on Silver Wraith, FLW 90, supplied to the Japanese Imperial Household and photographed at the Imperial Castle in Tokyo.

Built for Nubar Gulbenkian Esq., this special 4 door Cabriolet with power operated hood on a long wheelbase Silver Wraith, ALW 11, is body No. 9867, design No. 8335 and was used by Her Majesty the Queen when visiting Nigeria.

This two door Drop-head Coupé on Silver Wraith, WVH 37, body No. 9875, design No. 8372, has its radiator four inches forward of the normal line. It was exhibited at the Geneva Show in 1953. Below: Body No. 9892, design No. 8371, a Drop-head Coupé on Silver Wraith, WVH 40.

Another Geneva Show car of 1953. Named as a 4 door Drop-head Coupé, this body is number 9893 and design No. 8373, mounted on Silver Wraith, WVH 74.

The above car has been identified as body No. 9749, design No. 8381, a Limousine on Silver Wraith, BLW 15. It has an earlier type windscreen, bumper overriders, rear spat fixing and a higher roof line than the lower car which is a Touring Limousine, body No. 9936, design No. 8390 on Silver Wraith, LBLW 14. The problem is, the upper car has a body number nearly 200 earlier than the lower car but the chassis number is one later, it was delivered and photographed just after the lower car but is thought to be the prototype of design No. 8390.

The top photograph shows a Touring
Limousine, body No. 9957, design
No. 8390 on Silver Wraith, BLW 62.

The centre photograph is the interior
of the lower car on the opposite page
which was sent on show to America.

Below is body No. 10,000 another
Touring Limousine of design No.
8390. This car, Silver Wraith,
CLW 35, was built for the Amir of
Bahawalpur.

Design No. 8390 in a Autumnal setting.

The Silver Dawn version of design No. 8390, this is design No. 8401 actually taken from a much earlier Bentley Mark VI design.

A four light Touring Limousine, body No. 10107, design No. 8411 on Silver Wraith, ELW 82.

Slight modifications again with an amended rear of the body with larger quarter lights, a Limousine, body No. 10082, design No. 8420 on Silver Wraith, DLW 98.

Another four light Touring Limousine this time with a less happy wing line. Body No. 10062, design No. 8422 on Silver Wraith, DLW 133.

Design No. 8455 a Touring Limousine, the most obvious difference to design No. 8390 being the built-in headlights and chromium line on the wings. Body No. 10102 on Silver Wraith, FLW 5, exhibited on the Hooper stand at Earls Court in 1956.

Saloon, body No. 10114, design No. 8456 on Silver Wraith, LFLW 69.

Again a four light Touring Limousine, body No. 10110, design No. 8476 on Silver Wraith, FLW 42. Note the pre-war type door handles.

Above is design No. 8500, its difference to design No. 8455 is not readily apparent.
Body No. 10246, a Touring Limousine on Silver Wraith, GLW 12. Just to confuse matters
the lower car, Silver Wraith, FLW 99, body No. 10244 a Touring Limousine is another
of design 8500 but with an entirely different wing line to the above car.

The first of the Hooper Silver Cloud bodies is No. 10126, a Saloon, design No. 8535 on SWA 46, delivered in January 1956.

The lower car built for Sir James Cayzer is a Touring Limousine, body No. 10203, design No. 8444 on Silver Cloud, SDD 148.

Design No. 8504, Saloon with division. Most probably body No. 10223 on Silver Cloud, ALC 5, exhibited on the Hooper stand at Earls Court in 1957. Below with the alternative front wing/headlamp treatment is a Saloon, design No. 8523.

Although this appears to be a Silver Cloud design, it is in fact design No. 8516, body No. 10247 on Silver Wraith, GLW 14, delivered in April 1958.

A Two door Saloon, body No. 10283, design No. 8546 on Silver Cloud, BLC 35.

Design No. 8585 according to the photograph, or Design No. 8570 if one believes the Hooper Body Book, a four light Saloon with division, body No. 10267 on Silver Cloud II, LLCA 1, exhibited on the Hooper stand at Earls Court in 1959.

Silver Cloud, LSLG 78, originally a standard steel saloon, converted by Hoopers to a two door two seater Fixed-head Coupé.

Saloon with Perspex Top built for Nubar Gulbenkian Esq. Body No. 10175, design No. 8449 on Silver Wraith, LELW 74.

Below: Built for King Faisal of Iraq, a Drop-head Coupé on Silver Cloud, LSGE 252, body No. 10255, design No. 8530.

Four photographs showing the Allweather body supplied with a detachable perspex roof to H.M. King Paul of Hellenes. Body No. 10287, design No. 8537, on Silver Wraith, LHLW 44, delivered in March 1959.

Hoopers only production Phantom V body. A limousine, body No. 10262, design No. 8569 on 5 AS 19, registration No. YUW 280. This car was exhibited on the Hooper stand at Earls Court in 1959, the last show at which the company exhibited.

CHAPTER FOUR

H. J. MULLINER

From the parent company of Mulliners of Northampton and through the coachbuilding concern of A. G. Mulliner in Liverpool, emerged in 1900 the firm of H. J. Mulliner & Co. of Brook Street, Mayfair, London. H. J. Mulliner having purchased from his cousins the motor car body building section of Mulliner London Ltd., a joint venture of A. G. Mulliner of Liverpool and Arthur Mulliner of Northampton.

The company prospered, being closely identified with the leading makes of chassis and with Rolls-Royce from the commencement of that company.

To cope with growing business, additional premises were acquired in Bath Road, Chiswick, London, and showrooms were taken in Grafton Street, Mayfair.

Shortly before the First World War, H. J. Mulliner, wishing to retire, sold out to John Croall & Sons Ltd., an old-established Edinburgh firm of coachbuilders. The company continued under its old name and was managed by Mr. Frank Piesse, brother-in-law of H. J. Mulliner.

Between the wars, H. J. Mulliner & Co. constructed hundreds of fine bodies for mounting on Rolls-Royce chassis, their 1936-39 razor-edge saloons with thin windscreen pillars being particularly elegant.

After the Second World War coachbuilding continued but on a much reduced scale and in 1959 an approach was made to Rolls-Royce which resulted in that company taking over H. J. Mulliner & Co.

In 1961 Rolls-Royce Ltd., then merged their two coach-building companies, Park Ward and H. J. Mulliner into one entity under the name of H. J. Mulliner, Park Ward Ltd.

The Chiswick factory carried on until 1968 when the repairs and spares departments were transferred to the Rolls-Royce factory at Hythe Road, the production having been absorbed into the Willesden factory shortly after the merger.

Extracts from
H. J. Mulliner body book
referring to coachwork
mounted on Rolls-Royce
chassis only

JOB NO.	DESIGN NO.	CHASSIS	CHASSIS NO.	TYPE OF BODY	REMARKS	DELIVERY DATE
4728	7043	Silver Wraith	WAB 19	Touring Limousine		Oct. 1948
4730		Silver Wraith	WVA 30	Touring Saloon	Paris Salon 1947	Oct. 1947
4736	7019	Silver Wraith	WTA 1	Sedanca de Ville		Sept. 1946
4737	7019	Silver Wraith	WTA 9	Sedanca de Ville		Nov. 1946
4738	7019	Silver Wraith	WTA 29	Sedanca de Ville		Jan. 1947
4739	7019	Silver Wraith	WTA 25	Sedanca de Ville		Feb. 1947
4740	7019	Silver Wraith	WTA 52	Sedanca de Ville		Feb. 1947
4741	7055	Silver Wraith	WTA 64	Sedanca de Ville		May 1947
4742	7019	Silver Wraith	WTA 65	Sedanca de Ville		Apr. 1947
4743	7055	Silver Wraith	WTA 43	Sedanca de Ville		June 1947
4744	7055	Silver Wraith	WVA 7	Sedanca de Ville		Sept. 1947
4745	7055	Silver Wraith	WYA 77	Sedanca de Ville		May 1947
4746	7055	Silver Wraith	WYA 35	Sedanca de Ville		May 1948
4747	7019	Silver Wraith	WTA 66	Sedanca de Ville		May 1947
4748	7019	Silver Wraith	WTA 67	Sedanca de Ville		

JOB NO.	DESIGN NO.	CHASSIS	CHASSIS NO.	TYPE OF BODY	REMARKS	DELIVERY DATE
4749	7019	Silver Wraith	WTA 49	Sedanca de Ville		May 1947
4750	7019	Silver Wraith	WTA 51	Sedanca de Ville		
4751	7055	Silver Wraith	WVA 26	Sedanca de Ville		Aug. 1947
4752	7019	Silver Wraith	WTA 60	Sedanca de Ville		May 1947
4753	7055	Silver Wraith	WYA 28	Sedanca de Ville		Dec. 1947
4754	7055	Silver Wraith	WYA 59	Sedanca de Ville		Mar. 1948
4755	7019	Silver Wraith	WTA 57	Sedanca de Ville		June 1947
4756	7055	Silver Wraith	WVA 1	Sedanca de Ville		Nov. 1947
4757	7055	Silver Wraith	WYA 65	Sedanca de Ville		May 1948
4758	7055	Silver Wraith	WYA 11	Sedanca de Ville		Oct. 1947
4759		Silver Wraith	WYA 36	Long Limousine		Feb. 1948
4760	7055	Silver Wraith	WVA 79	Sedanca de Ville		Dec. 1947
4761	7019	Silver Wraith	WTA 72	Sedanca de Ville		June 1947
4796	7062	Silver Wraith	WDC 43	Saloon	With Division	Apr. 1949
4797	7062	Silver Wraith	WTA 75	Touring Limousine		Nov. 1947
4798	7064	Silver Wraith	WYA 12	Saloon		Nov. 1947
4799	7062	Silver Wraith	WAB 9	Touring Limousine	No Division	July 1948
4800	7062	Silver Wraith	WDC 10	Touring Limousine	Brussels Show	Dec. 1948
4801	7062	Silver Wraith	WVA 80	Touring Limousine		Nov. 1947
4802	7062	Silver Wraith	WTA 69	Touring Limousine		Oct. 1947
4805	7062	Silver Wraith	WYA 25	Touring Limousine		Jan. 1948
4856	7055	Silver Wraith	WYA 61	Sedanca de Ville		Feb. 1948
4857	7055	Silver Wraith	WZB 15	Sedanca de Ville		Apr. 1948
4858	7055	Silver Wraith	WAB 11	Sedanca de Ville		Aug. 1948
4859	7055	Silver Wraith	WZB 22	Sedanca de Ville		May 1948
4860	7055	Silver Wraith	WZB 60	Sedanca de Ville		July 1948
4861	7055	Silver Wraith	WZB 28	Sedanca de Ville		June 1948
4862	7055	Silver Wraith	WVA 37	Sedanca de Ville		Sept. 1947
4863	7055	Silver Wraith	WVA 8	Sedanca de Ville		June 1947
4864	7055	Silver Wraith	WCB 28	Sedanca de Ville		Oct. 1948
4865	7055	Silver Wraith	WCB 62	Sedanca de Ville		Jan. 1949
4866	7062	Silver Wraith	WYA 87	Touring Saloon	Geneva Show 1948	Feb. 1948
4867	7082	Silver Wraith	WTA 74	Enclosed Drive Limousine		Sept. 1947
4868	7042	Silver Wraith	WDC 22	Sedanca de Ville		Apr. 1949
4869	7062	Silver Wraith	WYA 49	Touring Limousine		Feb. 1948
4873	7062	Silver Wraith	WZB 6	Saloon		June 1948
4874	7062	Silver Wraith	WDC 41	Touring Limousine		Feb. 1949
4875	7081	Silver Wraith	WVA 36	Touring Limousine		Sept. 1947
4901	7062	Silver Wraith	WZB 14	Touring Limousine		Apr. 1948
4902	7127	Silver Wraith	WAB 27	Long Touring Limousine		Sept. 1948
4903	7055	Silver Wraith	WYA 2	Sedanca de Ville		
4904	7055	Silver Wraith	WYA 29	Sedanca de Ville		Feb. 1948
4905	7055	Silver Wraith	WCB 32	Sedanca de Ville		Dec. 1948
4906	7055	Silver Wraith	WZB 59	Sedanca de Ville		July 1948
4907	7055	Silver Wraith	WCB 55	Sedanca de Ville		Nov. 1948
4908	7055	Silver Wraith	WYA 32	Sedanca de Ville		Jan. 1948
4909	7055	Silver Wraith	WAB 20	Sedanca de Ville		Aug. 1948
4910	7055	Silver Wraith	WDC 26	Sedanca de Ville		Feb. 1949
4911	7055	Silver Wraith	WAB 26	Sedanca de Ville		Sept. 1948
4912	7055	Silver Wraith	WDC 68	Sedanca de Ville		Mar. 1949
4913	7055	Silver Wraith	WAB 42	Sedanca de Ville		Sept. 1948
4914	7055	Silver Wraith	WDC 35	Sedanca de Ville		Mar. 1949

JOB NO.	DESIGN NO.	CHASSIS	CHASSIS NO.	TYPE OF BODY	REMARKS	DELIVERY DATE
4915	7055	Silver Wraith	WCB 10	Sedanca de Ville	Earls Court Show 1948	Nov. 1948
4916	7055	Silver Wraith	WDC 78	Sedanca de Ville		May 1949
4917	7055	Silver Wraith	WCB 58	Sedanca de Ville		Dec. 1948
4918	7055	Silver Wraith	WCB 44	Sedanca de Ville		Jan. 1949
4919		Silver Wraith	WCB 72	Limousine		Jan. 1949
4920	7055	Silver Wraith	WAB 32	Sedanca de Ville		Sept. 1948
4921	7055	Silver Wraith	WCB 39	Sedanca de Ville		Nov. 1948
4922	7055	Silver Wraith	WDC 44	Sedanca de Ville		Feb. 1949
4923	7055	Silver Wraith	WDC 76	Sedanca de Ville		Jan. 1950
4924	7055	Silver Wraith	WDC 71	Sedanca de Ville		Feb. 1949
4925	7055	Silver Wraith	WDC 29	Sedanca de Ville		Feb. 1949
4926	7055	Silver Wraith	WDC 65	Sedanca de Ville		Mar. 1949
4927	7055	Silver Wraith	WDC 36	Sedanca de Ville		Feb. 1949
4928	7062	Silver Wraith	WAB 23	Limousine		Sept. 1948
4929	7062	Silver Wraith	WAB 3	Limousine		Aug. 1948
4930	7062	Silver Wraith	WZB 58	Limousine		June 1948
4932		Silver Wraith	WDC 83	Special Sedanca de Ville		July 1949
4933	7042	Silver Wraith	WZB 3	Sedanca de Ville		June 1949
4936	7062	Silver Wraith	WAB 43	Limousine		Sept. 1948
4937	7062	Silver Wraith	WDC 28	Saloon		Jan. 1949
4939	7249	Silver Wraith	WLE 12	Touring Limousine		Mar. 1951
4943	7062	Silver Wraith	WDC 62	Limousine		Mar. 1949
4944	7062	Silver Wraith	WDC 74	Limousine		Apr. 1949
4945	7183	Phantom IV	4AF 18	Cabriolet		Mar. 1952
4946	7062	Silver Wraith	WCB 30	Saloon		Oct. 1948
4948	7062	Silver Wraith	WDC 32	Saloon		Mar. 1949
4949	7118	Silver Wraith	WME 44	Saloon		May 1951
4952	7062	Silver Wraith	WYA 81	Touring Limousine		Feb. 1948
4953	7062	Silver Wraith	WZB 21	Touring Limousine		May 1948
4954	7062	Silver Wraith	WZB 27	Touring Limousine		June 1948
4955	7062	Silver Wraith	WAB 8	Touring Limousine		July 1948
4956	7062	Silver Wraith	W ?? 51	Touring Limousine		July 1949
4958	7062	Silver Wraith	WCB 69	Touring Limousine		Dec. 1948
4959	7062	Silver Wraith	WDC 79	Touring Limousine		Apr. 1949
4960	7062	Silver Wraith	WDC 17	Touring Limousine		Apr. 1949
4961	7062	Silver Wraith	WCB 66	Touring Limousine		Nov. 1948
4962	7136	Silver Wraith	WDC 46	Long Touring Limousine		Mar. 1949
4963	7135	Silver Wraith	WAB 2	Sedanca de Ville		Aug. 1948
4964	7062	Silver Wraith	WFC 40	Touring Limousine		July 1949
4965	7062	Silver Wraith	WAB 10	Touring Limousine		Aug. 1948
4966	7062	Silver Wraith	WDC 59	Touring Saloon		Apr. 1949
4967	7062	Silver Wraith	WDC 33	Touring Limousine		Jan. 1949
4968	7062	Silver Wraith	WAB 34	Touring Limousine		Sept. 1948
4969	7062	Silver Wraith	WCB 19	Touring Limousine	H.J.M. stand E.C. Show '48	Jan. 1949
4970	7062	Silver Wraith	WDC 3	Touring Limousine	Melbourne Show	Dec. 1948
4971	7062	Silver Wraith	WCB 31	Touring Limousine		Nov. 1948
4972	7062	Silver Wraith	WDC 96	Touring Limousine		May 1949
4973	7062	Silver Wraith	WAB 61	Touring Limousine	Paris Salon 1948	Sept. 1948
4974	7062	Silver Wraith	WDC 30	Touring Limousine	Geneva Show 1949	Mar. 1949
4975	7062	Silver Wraith	WGC 65	Saloon		Feb. 1950
4976	7062	Silver Wraith	WDC 97	Touring Limousine		May 1949
4981		Silver Wraith	WCB 17	Sedanca de Ville	H.J.M. stand E.C. Show '48	Dec. 1948

JOB NO.	DESIGN NO.	CHASSIS	CHASSIS NO.	TYPE OF BODY	REMARKS	DELIVERY DATE
4983	7144	Silver Wraith	WDC 23	Sedanca de Ville		Jan. 1949
4995	7055	Silver Wraith	WDC 82	Sedanca de Ville		May 1949
4997	7062	Silver Wraith	WGC 34	Touring Limousine		Nov. 1949
4998		Silver Wraith	WFC 49	Touring Saloon	Reg. No. UMC 71	July 1949
4999	7062	Silver Wraith	WDC 80	Touring Limousine		May 1949
5000	7062	Silver Wraith	WDC 81	Touring Limousine		May 1949
5001		Silver Wraith	WDC 52	Touring Saloon	Without division	Apr. 1949
5005	7062	Silver Wraith	WFC 16	Touring Saloon		May 1949
5006	7062	Silver Wraith	WFC 76	Touring Limousine		July 1949
5007	7062	Silver Wraith	WFC 57	Touring Limousine		Nov. 1949
5008	7062	Silver Wraith	WFC 90	Touring Limousine		July 1949
5009		Silver Wraith	WDC 101	Touring Saloon		May 1949
5010	7062	Silver Wraith	WGC 46	Touring Limousine		Apr. 1950
5012.	7062	Silver Wraith	WFC 41	Touring Saloon		July 1949
5013	7062	Silver Wraith	LWFC 65	Touring Limousine		June 1949
5014	7062	Silver Wraith	WDC 90	Touring Limousine		June 1949
5015		Silver Wraith	WZB 47	Sedanca de Ville		Oct. 1949
5016	7055	Silver Wraith	WFC 19	Sedanca de Ville		Sept. 1949
5017	7055	Silver Wraith	WFC 21	Sedanca de Ville		July 1949
5018	7055	Silver Wraith	WDC 89	Sedanca de Ville		May 1949
5019	7055	Silver Wraith	WDC 95	Sedanca de Ville		July 1949
5020		Silver Wraith	WFC 2	Sedanca de Ville		May 1949
5021	7055	Silver Wraith	WFC 28	Sedanca de Ville		July 1949
5022	7055	Silver Wraith	LWFC 95	Sedanca de Ville		Aug. 1949
5023	7055	Silver Wraith	WFC 61	Sedanca de Ville		Aug. 1949
5024	7055	Silver Wraith	WFC 74	Sedanca de Ville		Nov. 1949
5025		Silver Wraith	WFC 37	Touring Saloon		May 1949
5028	7042	Silver Wraith	WGC 38	Sedanca de Ville	Brussels Show	Jan. 1950
5031		Silver Wraith	LWHD 10	Sedanca de Ville		May 1950
5033	7062	Silver Wraith	WCB 15	Touring Limousine		Apr. 1949
5034	7162	Phantom IV	4 AF 2	Enclosed Drive Limousine		July 1950
5035	7181	Phantom IV	4 AF 14	Enclosed Drive Limousine		June 1952
5036	7181	Phantom IV	4 AF 16	Enclosed Drive Limousine		July 1952
5037	7062	Silver Wraith	WGC 30	Touring Saloon		Nov. 1949
5038	7062	Silver Wraith	WGC 67	Touring Saloon		Jan. 1950
5043		Silver Wraith	WFC 93	Touring Limousine		Aug. 1949
5044		Silver Wraith	WGC 3	Touring Limousine		Sept. 1949
5045	7062	Silver Wraith	WGC 60	Touring Limousine		Dec. 1949
5071	7171	Silver Wraith	WFC 82	Limousine		Oct. 1949
5076	As 4981	Silver Wraith	LWHD 12	Sedanca de Ville	New York Show	Mar. 1950
5077	7205	Phantom IV	4 AF 6	2 door, 4 light Cabriolet		Feb. 1951
5078		Silver Wraith	WGC 45	Special Long Limousine		Dec. 1949
5080		Silver Wraith	WLE 11	Limousine		Dec. 1950
5081	7062	Silver Wraith	WGC 43	Touring Limousine	Scottish Show 1949	Nov. 1949
5082		Silver Wraith	WFC 83	Touring Saloon		Aug. 1949
5083		Silver Wraith	WGC 29	Touring Limousine		Nov. 1949
5084	7062	Silver Wraith	WGC 8	Touring Limousine		Dec. 1949
5085	7062	Silver Wraith	WGC 14	Touring Limousine	Paris Salon	Sept. 1949
5086		Silver Wraith	WGC 69	Touring Limousine		Feb. 1950
5087	7062	Silver Wraith	WFC 101	Touring Limousine	H.J.M. stand E.C. Show '49	Oct. 1949
5088		Silver Wraith	WGC 68	Touring Limousine		Jan. 1950
5089	7062	Silver Wraith	WHD 18	Touring Limousine		June 1950

JOB NO.	DESIGN NO.	CHASSIS	CHASSIS NO.	TYPE OF BODY	REMARKS	DELIVERY DATE
5090	7062	Silver Wraith	WGC 75	Touring Limousine		Feb. 1950
5091	As 4981	Silver Wraith	LWGC 89	Limousine		Mar. 1950
5092	As 4981	Silver Wraith	LWGC 96	Limousine		Mar. 1950
5093		Silver Wraith	WGC 97	Touring Limousine		Apr. 1950
5094	7055	Silver Wraith	WFC 87	Sedanca de Ville		Sept. 1949
5095	7055	Silver Wraith	WGC 27	Sedanca de Ville		Dec. 1949
5096		Silver Wraith	LWGC 58	Sedanca de Ville		Dec. 1949
5097	7055	Silver Wraith	WGC 53	Sedanca de Ville		Jan. 1950
5098		Silver Wraith	WGC 62	Sedanca de Ville		Jan. 1950
5099	7055	Silver Wraith	WGC 72	Sedanca de Ville		Feb. 1950
5101	7171	Silver Wraith	WFC 25	Limousine		Oct. 1949
5102	7175/A	Silver Wraith	WGC 48	Drop Head Coupé	2 door	Feb. 1950
5104	7042	Silver Wraith	WGC 10	Sedanca de Ville	As Mdivani 4933	Oct. 1949
5106	As 4981	Silver Wraith	WFC 99	Sedanca de Ville	Possibly RR stand '49 Show	Sept. 1949
5107	7062	Silver Wraith	WGC 33	Touring Limousine		Dec. 1949
5108	7062	Silver Wraith	WGC 80	Touring Limousine		Mar. 1950
5109		Silver Wraith	WGC 82	Touring Limousine		Mar. 1950
5110	7062	Silver Wraith	WHD 3	Touring Limousine		Mar. 1950
5111	7062	Silver Wraith	WGC 98	Touring Limousine		May 1950
5112	7062	Silver Wraith	WHD 23	Touring Limousine		May 1950
5129		Silver Wraith	WHD 64	Touring Limousine		July 1950
5140	7062	Silver Wraith	LWHD 21	Touring Limousine		May 1950
5141	7062	Silver Wraith	WGC 100	Touring Limousine		May 1950
5142	7062	Silver Wraith	WHD 36	Touring Limousine		June 1950
5143	7062	Silver Wraith	WHD 45	Touring Limousine		July 1950
5144	7062	Silver Wraith	WHD 38	Touring Limousine		July 1950
5145	7062	Silver Wraith	WHD 75	Touring Limousine		Sept. 1950
5146	7062	Silver Wraith	WHD 51	Touring Limousine		July 1950
5147		Silver Wraith	WHD 61	Touring Limousine		Aug. 1950
5148		Silver Wraith	WHD 55	Touring Limousine		July 1950
5150	7062	Silver Wraith	WHD 6	Touring Limousine		June 1950
5151	7062	Silver Wraith	WHD 31	Touring Limousine		June 1950
5153	7206	Phantom IV	4 AF 8	6 light Saloon		July 1951
5154	7062	Silver Wraith	WHD 66	Limousine		July 1950
5155		Silver Wraith	LWHD 50	Limousine		July 1950
5156	7171	Silver Wraith	LWHD 48	Enclosed Drive Limousine		Aug. 1950
5157	7171	Silver Wraith	WLE 9	Enclosed Drive Limousine		Nov. 1950
5158	7171	Silver Wraith	WHD 69	Enclosed Drive Limousine		Sept. 1950
5159	7171	Silver Wraith	WHD 90	Enclosed Drive Limousine		Nov. 1950
5160	7171	Silver Wraith	LWLE 10	Enclosed Drive Limousine		Nov. 1950
5161	7171	Silver Wraith	LWLE 34	Enclosed Drive Limousine		Mar. 1951
5169	As 5028	Silver Wraith	WHD 35	Limousine		July 1950
5170	7118	Silver Wraith	WHD 71	Touring Limousine		Sept. 1950
5171	7118	Silver Wraith	WLE 7	Touring Limousine		Nov. 1950
5172	7118	Silver Wraith	WHD 76	Touring Limousine		Aug. 1950
5173	7118	Silver Wraith	WHD 100	Touring Limousine		Oct. 1950
5174	7118	Silver Wraith	WHD 101	Touring Limousine		Sept. 1950
5175	7118	Silver Wraith	WLE 32	Touring Limousine		Jan. 1951
5176	7118	Silver Wraith	LWME 6	Touring Limousine		Feb. 1951
5177	7118	Silver Wraith	WLE 25	Touring Limousine		Feb. 1951
5178	7118	Silver Wraith	WLE 35	Touring Limousine		Feb. 1951
5179	7118	Silver Wraith	WLE 2	Touring Saloon		Nov. 1950

JOB NO.	DESIGN NO.	CHASSIS	CHASSIS NO.	TYPE OF BODY	REMARKS	DELIVERY DATE
5190	7055	Silver Wraith	WHD 93	Sedanca de Ville		Oct. 1950
5191	7120	Silver Wraith	LWHD 97	Sedanca de Ville		Nov. 1950
5192	7120	Silver Wraith	WHD 88	Sedanca de Ville	H.J.M. stand E.C. Show '50	Nov. 1950
5193	7120	Silver Wraith	WHD 98	Sedanca de Ville		Dec. 1950
5194	7120	Silver Wraith	LWLE 16	Sedanca de Ville		Dec. 1950
5195	7120	Silver Wraith	LWLE 18	Sedanca de Ville	Fixed Head	Jan. 1951
5196	7120	Silver Wraith	WLE 24	Sedanca de Ville		Jan. 1951
5197	7120	Silver Wraith	LWLE 28	Sedanca de Ville		Jan. 1951
5198	7120	Silver Wraith	WME 26	Sedanca de Ville		Apr. 1951
5199	7120	Silver Wraith	WME 68	Sedanca de Ville		Aug. 1951
5200		Silver Wraith	WHD 89	Touring Limousine	Earls Court Show 1950	Nov. 1950
5201	7249	Silver Wraith	WLE 4	Touring Limousine		Dec. 1950
5204	7118	Silver Wraith	WME 12	Touring Limousine		Mar. 1951
5205	7118	Silver Wraith	WME 61	Touring Limousine		July 1951
5252	7249	Silver Wraith	WLE 30	Touring Limousine	Geneva Show 1951	Feb. 1951
5253	7249	Silver Wraith	WLE 21	Touring Limousine	Melbourne Show	Feb. 1951
5254	7254	Silver Wraith	WLE 31	Pullman Landaulette		Apr. 1951
5256	As 4981	Silver Wraith	LWME 34	Limousine		May 1951
5257	As 4981	Silver Wraith	LWME 31	Limousine		Aug. 1951
5258	As 4981	Silver Wraith	LWME 59	Limousine		Aug. 1951
5260	7249	Silver Wraith	WLE 8	Saloon		Mar. 1951
5261	7249	Silver Wraith	WME 4	Touring Limousine		Apr. 1951
5262	7171	Silver Wraith	LWME 23	Enclosed Drive Limousine		May 1951
5263	7249	Silver Wraith	WME 17	Touring Limousine		Apr. 1951
5264	7249	Silver Wraith	WME 11	Touring Limousine		Apr. 1951
5265	7249	Silver Wraith	WME 49	Touring Limousine	Festival of Britain 1951	Apr. 1951
5266	7258	Silver Wraith	WME 2	Enclosed Drive Limousine		Apr. 1951
5267	7258	Silver Wraith	WME 7	Enclosed Drive Limousine		Apr. 1951
5268	7258	Silver Wraith	WME 3	Enclosed Drive Limousine		Apr. 1951
5269	7258	Silver Wraith	WME 8	Enclosed Drive Limousine		May 1951
5270	7258	Silver Wraith	WME 24	Enclosed Drive Limousine		May 1951
5271	7258	Silver Wraith	WME 25	Enclosed Drive Limousine		May 1951
5272	7258	Silver Wraith	WME 48	Enclosed Drive Limousine		June 1951
5273	7258	Silver Wraith	WME 53	Enclosed Drive Limousine		June 1951
5274	7258	Silver Wraith	WME 57	Enclosed Drive Limousine		June 1951
5275	7258	Silver Wraith	WME 64	Enclosed Drive Limousine		June 1951
5276	7258	Silver Wraith	WME 63	Enclosed Drive Limousine		June 1951
5277	7171	Silver Wraith	WME 65	Enclosed Drive Limousine		June 1951
5279	7249	Silver Wraith	WME 66	Touring Limousine		July 1951
5280	7249	Silver Wraith	WME 78	Touring Limousine		Aug. 1951
5283	7171	Silver Wraith	WME 93	7 passenger Limousine		Sept. 1951
5284	7171	Silver Wraith	WME 95	7 passenger Limousine		Nov. 1951
5285	7171	Silver Wraith	WME 94	7 passenger Limousine		Oct. 1951
5306	7249	Silver Wraith	LWME 21	Touring Limousine		June 1951
5307	7249	Silver Wraith	LWME 50	Touring Saloon		May 1951
5308	7249	Silver Wraith	WME 42	Touring Limousine		Aug. 1951
5309	7249	Silver Wraith	LWME 71	Touring Limousine		Aug. 1951
5310	7249	Silver Wraith	WME 73	Touring Limousine		Aug. 1951
5311	7249	Silver Wraith	WME 74	Touring Limousine		Aug. 1951
5312	7249	Silver Wraith	WME 77	Touring Limousine		Oct. 1951
5313	7249	Silver Wraith	WME 79	Touring Limousine		Oct. 1951
5314	7249	Silver Wraith	WME 81	Touring Limousine		Oct. 1951

H. J. MULLINER

JOB NO.	DESIGN NO.	CHASSIS	CHASSIS NO.	TYPE OF BODY	REMARKS	DELIVERY DATE
5315	7249	Silver Wraith	WME 87	Touring Limousine		Oct. 1951
5316	7249	Silver Wraith	WME 96	Touring Limousine		Nov. 1951
5317	7249	Silver Wraith	WOF 7	Touring Limousine		Nov. 1951
5318	7249	Silver Wraith	WOF 8	Tonring Limousine		Oct. 1951
5319	7249	Silver Wraith	WOF 16	Touring Limousine		Oct. 1951
5320	7249	Silver Wraith	WOF 30	Touring Limousine		Dec. 1951
5321	7249	Silver Wraith	WOF 26	Touring Limousine		Dec. 1951
5322	7249	Silver Wraith	WOF 73	Touring Limousine		May 1952
5323	7249	Silver Wraith	WOF 64	Touring Limousine	No Division	May 1952
5324	7249	Silver Wraith	WOF 63	Touring Limousine		Feb. 1952
5325	7249	Silver Wraith	LWOF 27	Touring Limousine		Nov. 1951
5327	7276	Silver Wraith	ALW 1	Enclosed Drive Limousine		Dec. 1951
5328	7276	Silver Wraith	LALW 9	Enclosed Drive Limousine		Apr. 1952
5329	7280	Silver Wraith	LWOF 35	Enclosed Drive Limousine		Feb. 1952
5353	7276	Silver Wraith	ALW 2	Enclosed Drive Limousine		Mar. 1952
5354	7276	Silver Wraith	ALW 3	Enclosed Drive Limousine		Apr. 1952
5355	7276	Silver Wraith	ALW 4	Enclosed Drive Limousine		Mar. 1952
5356	7276	Silver Wraith	LALW 7	Enclosed Drive Limousine		Mar. 1952
5357	7276	Silver Wraith	ALW 6	Enclosed Drive Limousine		Feb. 1952
5358	7276	Silver Wraith	LALW 8	Enclosed Drive Limousine		Apr. 1952
5359	7276	Silver Wraith	ALW 46	Enclosed Drive Limousine		May 1953
5360	7276	Silver Wraith	LBLW 24	Enclosed Drive Limousine		July 1953
5361	7276	Silver Wraith	LALW 45	Enclosed Drive Limousine		Feb. 1953
5362	7276	Silver Wraith	LBLW 5	Enclosed Drive Limousine		June 1953
5363	7276	Silver Wraith	LBLW 27	Enclosed Drive Limousine		Aug. 1953
5364	7276	Silver Wraith	ALW 50	Enclosed Drive Limousine		June 1953
5365	7276	Silver Wraith	LBLW 26	Enclosed Drive Limousine		Aug. 1953
5366	7249	Silver Wraith	WOF 57	Touring Limousine		Feb. 1952
5367	7249	Silver Wraith	WSG 21	Touring Limousine		Aug. 1952
5368	7249	Silver Wraith	WSG 51	Touring Limousine		Sept. 1952
5369	7249	Silver Wraith	WOF 74	Touring Limousine		Feb. 1952
5370	7249	Silver Wraith	WSG 15	Touring Limousine		June 1952
5371	7249	Silver Wraith	WSG 26	Touring Limousine		Aug. 1952
5372	7249	Silver Wraith	WSG 49	Touring Limousine		Sept. 1952
5373	7249	Silver Wraith	WSG 30	Touring Limousine		Sept. 1952
5374	7249	Silver Wraith	WSG 50	Touring Limousine		Oct. 1952
5375	7249	Silver Wraith	LWSG 8	Touring Limousine		May 1952
5376	7249	Silver Wraith	WOF 62	Touring Limousine		Feb. 1952
5377	7249	Silver Wraith	WSG 12	Touring Limousine		Apr. 1952
5378	7249	Silver Wraith	LWSG 53	Touring Limousine		Dec. 1952
5379	7249	Silver Wraith	WSG 14	Touring Limousine		July 1952
5380	7249	Silver Wraith	WSG 42	Saloon		Sept. 1952
5381	7249	Silver Wraith	WSG 69	Touring Limousine		Nov. 1952
5382	7249	Silver Wraith	LWSG 73	Touring Limousine		Sept. 1952
5383	7249	Silver Wraith	WSG 61	Touring Limousine		Nov. 1952
5384	7249	Silver Wraith	WVH 10	Touring Limousine		Nov. 1952
5385	7249	Silver Wraith	LWSG 74	Touring Limousine		Jan. 1953
5429	7120	Silver Wraith	WSG 29	Sedanca de Ville		Sept. 1952
5430	7120	Silver Wraith	LWSG 43	Sedanca de Ville		Aug. 1952
5431	7120	Silver Wraith	WVH 94	Sedanca de Ville		Oct. 1953
5432	7120	Silver Wraith	WVH 93	Sedanca de Ville		Sept. 1953
5433	7120	Silver Wraith	WVH 95	Sedanca de Ville		Dec. 1953

JOB NO.	DESIGN NO.	CHASSIS	CHASSIS NO.	TYPE OF BODY	REMARKS	DELIVERY DATE
5434	7153	Silver Wraith	WSG 31	Sedanca de Ville		Sept. 1952
5437	7296	Silver Dawn	SHD 50	Drop Head Coupé	Jensen Rear Window	Nov. 1952
5438	7311	Silver Wraith	LALW 29	7 passenger Cabriolet		Mar. 1953
5440	7310	Silver Wraith	LALW 27	7 passenger Limousine		Dec. 1952
5441	7281	Silver Wraith	ALW 32	Pullman Landaulette		Dec. 1952
5442	7297	Silver Dawn	LSLE 31	Drop Head Coupé		May 1953
5446	7276	Silver Wraith	LALW 16	Enclosed Drive Limousine		May 1952
5447	7276	Silver Wraith	LALW 17	Enclosed Drive Limousine		June 1952
5448	7276	Silver Wraith	LALW 18	Enclosed Drive Limousine		July 1952
5449	7276	Silver Wraith	ALW 12	Enclosed Drive Limousine		July 1952
5450	7276	Silver Wraith	ALW 15	Enclosed Drive Limousine		Sept. 1952
5451	7276	Silver Wraith	ALW 19	Enclosed Drive Limousine		July 1952
5452	7276	Silver Wraith	LALW 22	Enclosed Drive Limousine	Toronto Show	July 1952
5453	7276	Silver Wraith	LALW 26	Enclosed Drive Limousine		Oct. 1952
5454	7276	Silver Wraith	LALW 36	Enclosed Drive Limousine		Dec. 1952
5455	7276	Silver Wraith	ALW 20	Enclosed Drive Limousine		Nov. 1952
5456	7276	Silver Wraith	ALW 21	Enclosed Drive Limousine		Oct. 1952
5457	7276	Silver Wraith	LALW 25	Enclosed Drive Limousine		Oct. 1952
5458	7276	Silver Wraith	ALW 24	Enclosed Drive Limousine		Dec. 1952
5459	7276	Silver Wraith	ALW 28	Enclosed Drive Limousine		Sept. 1952
5460	7276	Silver Wraith	LALW 30	Enclosed Drive Limousine		Jan. 1953
5461	7276	Silver Wraith	LALW 34	Enclosed Drive Limousine	Earls Court Show	Dec. 1953
5462	7276	Silver Wraith	ALW 44	Enclosed Drive Limousine	Geneva Show 1953	Feb. 1953
5463	7276	Silver Wraith	ALW 51	Enclosed Drive Limousine		Apr. 1953
5464	7276	Silver Wraith	LALW 43	Enclosed Drive Limousine		Feb. 1953
5465	7276	Silver Wraith	ALW 38	Enclosed Drive Limousine		Feb. 1953
5490	7249	Silver Wraith	WVH 31	Touring Limousine		Jan. 1953
5491	7249	Silver Wraith	WVH 27	Touring Limousine		Nov. 1952
5492	7249	Silver Wraith	WVH 24	Touring Limousine		Dec. 1952
5493	7249	Silver Wraith	WVH 14	Touring Limousine		Dec. 1952
5494	7249	Silver Wraith	WVH 34	Saloon		Dec. 1952
5495	7249	Silver Wraith	WVH 47	Touring Limousine		Mar. 1953
5496	7249	Silver Wraith	WVH 45	Saloon		Feb. 1953
5497	7249	Silver Wraith	WVH 20	Touring Limousine		Jan. 1953
5498	7249	Silver Wraith	WVH 50	Touring Limousine		Feb. 1953
5499	7249	Silver Wraith	WVH 59	Touring Limousine		Feb. 1953
5500	7249	Silver Wraith	LWVH 57	Touring Limousine		Mar. 1953
5501	7249	Silver Wraith	WVH 68	Touring Limousine		May 1953
5502	7249	Silver Wraith	WVH 60	Touring Limousine		Mar. 1953
5503	7249	Silver Wraith	WVH 75	Touring Limousine		May 1953
5504	7249	Silver Wraith	LWVH 76	Touring Limousine		Mar. 1953
5505	7249	Silver Wraith	WVH 73	Touring Limousine		May 1953
5506	7249	Silver Wraith	WVH 67	Touring Limousine		Apr. 1953
5507	7249	Silver Wraith	WVH 85	Touring Limousine		June 1953
5508	7249	Silver Wraith	WVH 80	Touring Limousine		June 1953
5509	7249	Silver Wraith	LWVH 86	Touring Limousine		Apr. 1953
5526	7276	Silver Wraith	LBLW 8	Enclosed Drive Limousine		July 1953
5527	7276	Silver Wraith	LBLW 7	Enclosed Drive Limousine		July 1953
5528	7276	Silver Wraith	BLW 32	Enclosed Drive Limousine		Aug. 1953
5529	7276	Silver Wraith	LALW 48	Enclosed Drive Limousine		Apr. 1953
5530	7281	Silver Wraith	BLW 10	Pullman Landaulette		July 1953
5531	7276	Silver Wraith	LBLW 3	Enclosed Drive Limousine		July 1953

H. J. MULLINER

JOB NO.	DESIGN NO.	CHASSIS	CHASSIS NO.	TYPE OF BODY	REMARKS	DELIVERY DATE
5532	7276	Silver Wraith	LBLW 34	Enclosed Drive Limousine		Sept. 1953
5533	7276	Silver Wraith	LBLW 38	Enclosed Drive Limousine		Aug. 1953
5534	7276	Silver Wraith	BLW 20	Enclosed Drive Limousine		Oct. 1953
5536	7249	Silver Wraith	WVH 92	Touring Limousine		July 1953
5537	7249	Silver Wraith	WVH 107	Touring Limousine		Dec. 1953
5538	7249	Silver Wraith	WVH 96	Touring Limousine		Sept. 1953
5539	7249	Silver Wraith	WVH 103	Touring Limousine		Sept. 1953
5540	7249	Silver Wraith	LWVH 114	Touring Limousine		Nov. 1953
5570	7334	Silver Wraith	LWVH 90	Sedanca de Ville		May 1953
5581	7347	Silver Wraith	LBLW 37	7 passenger Cabriolet		Nov. 1953
5585	7356	Silver Wraith	LBLW 44	Touring Limousine		—
5591	7276	Silver Wraith	LBLW 35	Enclosed Drive Limousine		Dec. 1953
5592	7276	Silver Wraith	BLW 40	Enclosed Drive Limousine		Dec. 1953
5593	7276	Silver Wraith	BLW 41	Enclosed Drive Limousine		Jan. 1954
5608	7348	Silver Wraith	BLW 55	Sports Limousine	Earls Court Show 1953	Nov. 1953
5609	7358	Silver Wraith	LBLW 53	Enlcosed Drive Limousine	H.J.M. stand E.C. Show '53	Nov. 1953
5610	7358	Silver Wraith	BLW 56	Enclosed Drive Limousine		Nov. 1953
5611	7358	Silver Wraith	LBLW 89	Enclosed Drive Limousine		Mar. 1954
5612	7358	Silver Wraith	LBLW 68	Enclosed Drive Limousine		Apr. 1954
5613	7358	Silver Wraith	CLW 11	Enclosed Drive Limousine		Apr. 1954
5614	7358	Silver Wraith	DLW 51	Enclosed Drive Limousine		Nov. 1954
5625	7356	Silver Wraith	BLW 48	Touring Limousine	E.C. & Scottish Show '53	Nov. 1953
5626	7356	Silver Wraith	BLW 60	Touring Limousine	Earls Court Show 1953	Oct. 1953
5627	7356	Silver Wraith	LBLW 90	Touring Limousine		Jan. 1954
5628	7338	Silver Wraith	LBLW 45	Touring Limousine		Jan. 1954
5629	7356	Silver Wraith	LBLW 73	Touring Limousine		Feb. 1954
5630	7356	Silver Wraith	LBLW 91	Touring Limousine		Mar. 1954
5631	7356	Silver Wraith	LCLW 3	Touring Limousine		Mar. 1954
5632	7356	Silver Wraith	CLW 10	Touring Limousine		Apr. 1954
5633	7356	Silver Wraith	CLW 43	Touring Limousine		June 1954
5634	7348	Silver Wraith	LBLW 46	Sports Limousine		Dec. 1953
5635	7348	Silver Wraith	CLW 41	Sports Limousine		Aug. 1954
5636	7348	Silver Wraith	CLW 38	Sports Limousine		July 1954
5637	7348	Silver Wraith	DLW 10	Sports Limousine	Remounted HLW 7 Apr. '58	Oct. 1954
5638	7348	Silver Wraith	DLW 36	Sports Limousine		Sept. 1954
5639	7348	Silver Wraith	DLW 56	Sports Limousine	H.J.M. stand E.C. Show '54	Nov. 1954
5675	7356	Silver Wraith	CLW 26	Touring Limousine		May 1954
5676	7356	Silver Wraith	CLW 17	Touring Limousine		June 1954
5677	7356	Silver Wraith	CLW 23	Touring Limousine		Apr. 1954
5678	7356	Silver Wraith	DLW 2	Touring Limousine		July 1954
5679	7356	Silver Wraith	DLW 35	Touring Limousine		Sept. 1954
5680	7356	Silver Wraith	LDLW 20	Touring Limousine		Oct. 1954
5681	7356	Silver Wraith	LDLW 23	Touring Limousine		Aug. 1954
5682	7356	Silver Wraith	DLW 4	Touring Limousine		Aug. 1954
5683	7369	Silver Wraith	DLW 30	Saloon		Sept. 1954
5684	7356	Silver Wraith	CLW 24	Touring Limousine		June 1954
5685	7356	Silver Wraith	DLW 31	Touring Limousine		Sept. 1954
5686	7368	Phantom IV	4 BP 7	Enclosed Drive Limousine		July 1954
5694	7358	Silver Wraith	DLW 90	Enclosed Drive Limousine		Jan. 1955
5695	7358	Silver Wraith	DLW 93	Enclosed Drive Limousine		Feb. 1955
5696	7358	Silver Wraith	LELW 99	Enclosed Drive Limousine		Apr. 1956
5697	7358	Silver Wraith	DLW 124	Enclosed Drive Limousine		May 1955

JOB NO.	DESIGN NO.	CHASSIS	CHASSIS NO.	TYPE OF BODY	REMARKS	DELIVERY DATE
5716	7356	Silver Wraith	DLW 65	Touring Limousine		Nov. 1954
5717	7356	Silver Wraith	LDLW 42	Touring Limousine		Oct. 1954
5718	7356	Silver Wraith	LDLW 40	Touring Limousine		Sept. 1954
5719	7356	Silver Wraith	LDLW 28	Touring Limousine		Sept. 1954
5720	7356	Silver Wraith	DLW 46	Touring Limousine	R.R. stand E.C. Show 1954	Nov. 1954
5721	7348	Silver Wraith	DLW 57	Sports Limousine		Nov. 1954
5722	7348	Silver Wraith	DLW 73	Sports Limousine		Jan. 1955
5723	7348	Silver Wraith	DLW 82	Sports Limousine		Feb. 1955
5724	7376	Phantom IV	4 CS 2	Limousine		Nov. 1955
5725	7376	Phantom IV	4 CS 4	Limousine		Aug. 1955
5747	7243	Silver Dawn	LSVJ 133	Lightweight Saloon		May 1955
5770	7356	Silver Wraith	DLW 63	Touring Limousine		Dec. 1954
5771	7356	Silver Wraith	DLW 70	Touring Limousine		Dec. 1954
5772	7356	Silver Wraith	LDLW 67	Touring Limousine		Jan. 1955
5773	7356	Silver Wraith	LDLW 84	Touring Limousine		Feb. 1955
5774	7356	Silver Wraith	DLW 91	Touring Limousine		Apr. 1955
5775	7356	Silver Wraith	DLW 95	Touring Limousine		June 1955
5776	7356	Silver Wraith	DLW 96	Touring Limousine		Mar. 1955
5777	7356	Silver Wraith	DLW 97	Touring Limousine		Mar. 1955
5778	7356	Silver Wraith	LDLW 131	Touring Limousine		May 1955
5779	7356	Silver Wraith	DLW 99	Touring Limousine		Mar. 1955
5780	7356	Silver Wraith	LDLW 118	Touring Limousine		Mar. 1955
5781	7356	Silver Wraith	DLW 123	Touring Limousine		Apr. 1955
5782	7356	Silver Wraith	DLW 157	Touring Limousine		May 1955
5783	7356	Silver Wraith	DLW 172	Touring Limousine		July 1955
5794	7348	Silver Wraith	DLW 132	Sports Limousine		June 1955
5795	7348	Silver Wraith	DLW 129	Sports Limousine		June 1955
5796	7348	Silver Wraith	DLW 145	Sports Limousine		May 1955
5797	7348	Silver Wraith	ELW 45	Sports Limousine		Jan. 1956
5798	7348	Silver Wraith	FLW 3	Sports Limousine		Oct. 1956
5800	7358	Silver Wraith	LELW 49	Enclosed Drive Limousine		Mar. 1956
5801	7358	Silver Wraith	LELW 77	Enclosed Drive Limousine		May 1956
5802	7358	Silver Wraith	LELW 87	Enclosed Drive Limousine		July 1956
5803	7358	Silver Wraith	LELW 100	Enclosed Drive Limousine		Sept. 1956
5804	7358	Silver Wraith	LFLW 19	Enclosed Drive Limousine	H.J.M. stand E.C. Show '56	Nov. 1956
5815	7356	Silver Wraith	LDLW 166	Touring Limousine		July 1955
5816	7356	Silver Wraith	LCLW 9	Touring Limousine		May 1955
5817	7356	Silver Wraith	LDLW 165	Touring Limousine		July 1955
5818	7356	Silver Wraith	ELW 10	Touring Limousine		Nov. 1955
5819	7356	Silver Wraith	ELW 36	Touring Limousine		Nov. 1955
5826	7356	Silver Wraith	LELW 83	Touring Limousine		Feb. 1956
5827	7356	Silver Wraith	ELW 64	Touring Limousine		Mar. 1956
5828	7356	Silver Wraith	ELW 14	Touring Limousine	H.J.M. stand E.C. Show '55	Nov. 1955
5829	7356	Silver Wraith	LELW 84	Touring Saloon		Mar. 1956
5830	7356	Silver Wraith	ELW 65	Touring Limousine		Apr. 1956
5831	7348	Silver Wraith	LELW 24	Sports Limousine		Dec. 1955
5832	7348	Silver Wraith	ELW 5	Sports Limousine		Nov. 1955
5833	7348	Silver Wraith	ELW 17	Sports Limousine		Nov. 1955
5834	7348	Silver Wraith	FLW 29	Sports Limousine		Nov. 1955
5835	7348	Silver Wraith	ELW 47	Sports Limousine		May 1956
5841	7356	Silver Wraith	ELW 79	Touring Limousine		June 1956
5842	7356	Silver Wraith	LELW 28	Touring Limousine		Dec. 1955

H. J. MULLINER

JOB. NO.	DESIGN NO.	CHASSIS	CHASSIS NO.	TYPE OF BODY	REMARKS	DELIVERY DATE
5843	7356	Silver Wraith	LELW 81	Touring Limousine		July 1956
5844	7356	Silver Wraith	LFLW 22	Touring Limousine	Paris Salon 1956	Sept. 1956
5845	7356	Silver Wraith	ELW 50	Touring Limousine		Feb. 1956
5897	7356	Silver Wraith	LELW 85	Touring Limousine		Mar. 1956
5898	7356	Silver Wraith	LELW 92	Touring Limousine		July 1956
5899	7356	Silver Wraith	LELW 101	Touring Limousine		Sept. 1956
5900	7356	Silver Wraith	LELW 97	Touring Limousine		
5901	7356	Silver Wraith	FLW 18	Touring Limousine	R.R. stand E.C. Show 1956	Nov. 1956
5902	7356	Silver Wraith	FLW 37	Touring Limousine		Dec. 1956
5903	7356	Silver Wraith	FLW 72	Touring Limousine		Jan. 1957
5904	7356	Silver Wraith	FLW 27	Touring Limousine		Feb. 1957
5905	7356	Silver Wraith	FLW 49	Touring Limousine		Feb. 1957
5906	7356	Silver Wraith	ELW 50	Touring Limousine		Mar. 1957
5911	7412	Silver Cloud	SWA 76	Touring Saloon		Apr. 1956
5914	7412	Silver Cloud	SWA 94	Touring Saloon		May 1956
5921	7405	Silver Cloud	LSWA 62	Drop Head Coupé		Apr. 1956
5931	7416	Silver Cloud	LSWA 106	Drop Head Coupé		Apr. 1956
5993	7413	Silver Cloud	LSWA 104	Drop Head Coupé		Sept. 1956
5997	7410	Silver Cloud	LSZB 247	Drop Head Coupé	H.J.M. stand E.C. Show '56	Nov. 1956
5998	7410	Silver Cloud	SBC 118	Drop Head Coupé		
6003	7412	Silver Cloud	SYB 30	Saloon		Jan. 1957
6004	7412	Silver Cloud	SYB 162	Saloon		Jan. 1957
6009	7358	Silver Wraith	LFLW 79	Enclosed Drive Limousine		May 1957
6010	7358	Silver Wraith	LGLW 9	Enclosed Drive Limousine		Mar. 1958
6011	7358	Silver Wraith	LFLW 83	Enclosed Drive Limousine		June 1957
6012	7358	Silver Wraith	LGLW 8	Enclosed Drive Limousine		Mar. 1958
6013	7358	Silver Wraith	GLW 11	Enclosed Drive Limousine		Mar. 1958
6014	7356	Silver Wraith	FLW 52	Touring Limousine		Apr. 1957
6015	7356	Silver Wraith	LFLW 70	Touring Limousine		Mar. 1957
6016	7356	Silver Wraith	FLW 33	Touring Limousine		May 1957
6017	7356	Silver Wraith	FLW 54	Touring Limousine		May 1957
6018	7356	Silver Wraith	LFLW 84	Touring Limousine		June 1957
6040	7410	Silver Cloud	SCC 95	Drop Head Coupé		
6041	7410	Silver Cloud	SDD 194	Drop Head Coupé		
6042	7410	Silver Cloud	LSDD 146	Drop Head Coupé		
6048	7356	Silver Wraith	LFLW 95	Touring Limousine		Aug. 1957
6049	7356	Silver Wraith	FLW 100	Touring Limousine	H.J.M. stand E.C. Show '57	Nov. 1957
6050	7356	Silver Wraith	FLW 101	Touring Limousine	Paris Salon 1957	Sept. 1957
6051	7356	Silver Wraith	GLW 1	Touring Limousine		Nov. 1957
6052	7356	Silver Wraith	GLW 5	Touring Limousine		Apr. 1958
6053	7410	Silver Cloud	LSDD 302	Drop Head Coupé		May 1957
6054	7410	Silver Cloud	LSED 193	Drop Head Coupé		Sept. 1957
6062	7458	Silver Cloud	LSED 91	Fixed Head Coupé		Oct. 1957
6073	7410	Silver Cloud	LSED 345	Drop Head Coupé		
6074	7410	Silver Cloud		Drop Head Coupé		Nov. 1957
6076	7410	Silver Cloud	SED 257	Drop Head Coupé		
6077	7410	Silver Cloud	LSFE 449	Drop Head Coupé		
6083	7356	Silver Wraith	LGLW 7	Touring Limousine		Feb. 1958
6084	7356	Silver Wraith	LHLW 18	Touring Limousine		Sept. 1958
6085	7356	Silver Wraith	LHLW 21	Touring Limousine		Sept. 1958
6086	7356	Silver Wraith	LGLW 26	Touring Limousine		May 1958
6087	7356	Silver Wraith	LHLW 52	Touring Limousine		Feb. 1959

JOB NO.	DESIGN NO.	CHASSIS	CHASSIS NO.	TYPE OF BODY	REMARKS	DELIVERY DATE
6118	7410	Silver Cloud	LSFE 451	Drop Head Coupé		
6120	7410	Silver Cloud	SGE 40	Drop Head Coupé		May 1958
6121	7410	Silver Cloud	LSFE 483	Drop Head Coupé		
6122	7410	Silver Cloud	LSGE 210	Drop Head Coupé		
6123	7358	Silver Wraith	LGLW 23	Enclosed Drive Limousine		June 1958
6124	7358	Silver Wraith	GLW 22	Enclosed Drive Limousine		July 1958
6125	7358	Silver Wraith	LHLW 3	Enclosed Drive Limousine		Aug. 1958
6141	7358	Silver Wraith	HLW 24	Enclosed Drive Limousine		Oct. 1958
6142	7358	Silver Wraith	LHLW 22	Enclosed Drive Limousine		Sept. 1958
6143	7358	Silver Wraith	LHLW 23	Enclosed Drive Limousine		Nov. 1958
6144	7410	Silver Cloud	SGE 310	Drop Head Coupé		Sept. 1958
6145	7410	Silver Cloud	SGE 482	Drop Head Coupé		Nov. 1958
6146	7410	Silver Cloud	LSGE 492	Drop Head Coupé		Nov. 1958
6162	7358	Silver Wraith	LHLW 27	Enclosed Drive Limousine		Nov. 1958
6164	7493	Silver Wraith	LHLW 36	Enclosed Drive Limousine		Nov. 1958
6165	7415	Silver Cloud	LSGE 466	Drop Head Coupé		
6166	7410	Silver Cloud	LSJF 204	Drop Head Coupé		
C6173	7504	Silver Cloud	LSJF 60	Drop Head Coupé		
6174	7358	Silver Wraith	HLW 45	Enclosed Drive Limousine		Dec. 1958
6175	7358	Silver Wraith	HLW 46	Enclosed Drive Limousine		Dec. 1958
6176	7358	Silver Wraith	HLW 48	Enclosed Drive Limousine		Dec. 1958
6177	7358	Silver Wraith	HLW 50	Enclosed Drive Limousine		Dec. 1958
6191	7410	Silver Cloud	SKG 33	Drop Head Coupé		
6192	7410	Silver Cloud	SKG 31	Drop Head Coupé		
6199	7515	Phantom V	5 LAS 3	Limousine	H.J.M. stand E.C. Show '59 New York Show	Feb. 1960
C6200	7504	Silver Cloud	LSLG 110	Drop Head Coupé		
C6201	7504	Silver Cloud	LSLG 114	Drop Head Coupé		
C6203	7504	Silver Cloud	LSMH 21	Drop Head Coupé		
C6204	7504	Silver Cloud	LSMH 57	Drop Head Coupé		
C6205	7504	Silver Cloud	SMH 129	Drop Head Coupé		
EC6206	7503	Silver Cloud	LCLC 38	Radford Estate		
EC6207	7501	Silver Cloud	LCLG 112	Radford Estate		
EC6208	7506	Silver Cloud	LSMH 65	Radford Estate		
C6209	7504	Silver Cloud	LSMH 169	Drop Head Coupé		
C6210	7504	Silver Cloud	LSMH 207	Drop Head Coupé		
C6211	7504	Silver Cloud	LSMH 195	Drop Head Coupé		
C6212	7504	Silver Cloud	LSMH 245	Drop Head Coupé		
C6213	7504	Silver Cloud	SNH 14	Drop Head Coupé		
C6214	7504	Silver Cloud	LSNH 40	Drop Head Coupé		
C6216	7504	Silver Cloud	SNH 106	Drop Head Coupé		
C6217	7504	Silver Cloud	SPA 108	Drop Head Coupé		
C6218	7504	Silver Cloud	LSPA 258	Drop Head Coupé		
C6219	7504	Silver Cloud	LSPA 260	Drop Head Coupé		
EC6220	7503	Silver Cloud	LCLC 42	Radford Estate		
C6223	7504	Silver Cloud	LSRA 19	Drop Head Coupé		
C6225	7504	Silver Cloud	LSRA 139	Drop Head Coupé		
C6226	7504	Silver Cloud	LSRA 245	Drop Head Coupé		
C6227	7504	Silver Cloud	LSRA 295	Drop Head Coupé		
C6228	7504	Silver Cloud	LSRA 309	Drop Head Coupé		
C6229	7504	Silver Cloud	LSTB 28	Drop Head Coupé		
C6230	7504	Silver Cloud	STB 88	Drop Head Coupé		
C6251	7504	Silver Cloud	LSTB 172	Drop Head Coupé		

H. J. MULLINER

JOB NO.	DESIGN NO.	CHASSIS	CHASSIS NO.	TYPE OF BODY	REMARKS	DELIVERY DATE
C6253	7504	Silver Cloud	STB 190	Drop Head Coupé		
C6254	7504	Silver Cloud	LSTB 278	Drop Head Coupé		
C6255	7504	Silver Cloud	LSTB 298	Drop Head Coupé		
C6256	7504	Silver Cloud	LSTB 324	Drop Head Coupé		
C6257	7504	Silver Cloud	LSTB 366	Drop Head Coupé		
C6258	7504	Silver Cloud	STB 410	Drop Head Coupé		
C6259	7504	Silver Cloud	STB 444	Drop Head Coupé		
C6260	7504	Silver Cloud	LSVB 27	Drop Head Coupé		
C6261	7504	Silver Cloud	SVB 99	Drop Head Coupé		
C6262	7504	Silver Cloud	SVB 63	Drop Head Coupé		
C6263	7504	Silver Cloud	SVB 143	Drop Head Coupé		
C6330	7504	Silver Cloud	LSVB 269	Drop Head Coupé		
C6331	7504	Silver Cloud	LSVB 319	Drop Head Coupé		
C6332	7504	Silver Cloud	LSVB 369	Drop Head Coupé		
C6334	7504	Silver Cloud	LSVB 451	Drop Head Coupé		
C6336	7504	Silver Cloud	LSWC 68	Drop Head Coupé		
C6337	7504	Silver Cloud	SWC 122	Drop Head Coupé		
C6338	7504	Silver Cloud	LSWC 148	Drop Head Coupé	H.J.M. stand E.C. Show '60	
C6339	7504	Silver Cloud	SWC 178	Drop Head Coupé		
C6340	7504	Silver Cloud	LSWC 278	Drop Head Coupé		
C6341	7504	Silver Cloud	LSWC 230	Drop Head Coupé		
C6343	7504	Silver Cloud	LSWC 418	Drop Head Coupé		
6345	7516	Phantom V	5 AS 93	Limousine	R.R. stand E.C. Show 1960	Jan. 1961
6365	7484	Silver Cloud	LLCB 16	Cabriolet		May 1961
C6386	7504	Silver Cloud	LSWC 510	Drop Head Coupé		
C6387	7504	Silver Cloud	LSWC 524	Drop Head Coupé		
C6388	7504	Silver Cloud	LSWC 596	Drop Head Coupé		
C6390	7504	Silver Cloud	LSWC 680	Drop Head Coupé		
C6392	7504	Silver Cloud	LSWC 730	Drop Head Coupé		
C6393	7504	Silver Cloud	LSXC 67	Drop Head Coupé		
C6394	7504	Silver Cloud	SXC 123	Drop Head Coupé		
C6395	7504	Silver Cloud	LSXC 173	Drop Head Coupé	New York Show	
C6396	7504	Silver Cloud	SXC 277	Drop Head Coupé		
C6398	7504	Silver Cloud	LSXC 323	Drop Head Coupé		
C6399	7504	Silver Cloud	LSXC 359	Drop Head Coupé		
C6401	7504	Silver Cloud	SXC 465	Drop Head Coupé		
C6402	7504	Silver Cloud	SXC 521	Drop Head Coupé		
C6405	7504	Silver Cloud	LSXC 605	Drop Head Coupé		
C6406	7504	Silver Cloud	SYD 8	Drop Head Coupé		
C6407	7504	Silver Cloud	SYD 118	Drop Head Coupé		
C6408	7504	Silver Cloud	SXC 632	Drop Head Coupé		
C6409	7504	Silver Cloud	LSYD 46	Drop Head Coupé		
C6410	7504	Silver Cloud	LSYD 78	Drop Head Coupé		
6446	7516	Phantom V	5 LAT 86	Limousine		Jan. 1961
6447	7516	Phantom V	5 LAT 82	Limousine		May 1961
6448	7516	Phantom V	5 LBV 77	Limousine	No Division	
6449	7516	Phantom V	5 BV 93	Limousine		
6450	7516	Phantom V	5 LBX 14	Limousine		
6451	7516	Phantom V	5 LBX 48	Limousine		
6452	7516	Phantom V	5 LBX 90	Limousine		
C6466	7504	Silver Cloud	LSYD 150	Drop Head Coupé		
C6468	7504	Silver Cloud	SYD 188	Drop Head Coupé		

H. J. MULLINER

JOB NO.	DESIGN NO.	CHASSIS	CHASSIS NO.	TYPE OF BODY	REMARKS	DELIVERY DATE
C6470	7504	Silver Cloud	LSYD 218	Drop Head Coupé		
C6471	7504	Silver Cloud	LSYD 260	Drop Head Coupé		
C6472	7504	Silver Cloud	SYD 288	Drop Head Coupé		
C6473	7504	Silver Cloud	SYD 310	Drop Head Coupé		
C6475	7504	Silver Cloud	LSYD 334	Drop Head Coupé		
C6476	7504	Silver Cloud	LSYD 366	Drop Head Coupé		
C6477	7504	Silver Cloud	LSYD 390	Drop Head Coupé		
C6478	7504	Silver Cloud	LSYD 428	Drop Head Coupé		
C6479	7504	Silver Cloud	SYD 486	Drop Head Coupé		
C6480	7504	Silver Cloud	LSYD 456	Drop Head Coupé		
C6481	7504	Silver Cloud	LSZD 11	Drop Head Coupé		
C6482	7504	Silver Cloud	SZD 43	Drop Head Coupé		
C6483	7504	Silver Cloud	LSZD 53	Drop Head Coupé		
C6484	7504	Silver Cloud	LSZD 67	Drop Head Coupé		
C6485	7504	Silver Cloud	SZD 79	Drop Head Coupé		
C6516	7504	Silver Cloud	SZD 101	Drop Head Coupé		
C6517	7504	Silver Cloud	LSZD 115	Drop Head Coupé		
C6518	7504	Silver Cloud	LSZD 135	Drop Head Coupé		
C6519	7504	Silver Cloud	LSZD 161	Drop Head Coupé		
C6520	7504	Silver Cloud	LSZD 483	Drop Head Coupé		
C6521	7504	Silver Cloud	SZD 373	Drop Head Coupé		
C6522	7504	Silver Cloud	LSZD 355	Drop Head Coupé		
C6523	7504	Silver Cloud	LSZD 381	Drop Head Coupé		
C6524	7504	Silver Cloud	SZD 311	Drop Head Coupé		
C6525	7504	Silver Cloud	LSZD 395	Drop Head Coupé		
C6526	7504	Silver Cloud	SZD 415	Drop Head Coupé		
C6527	7504	Silver Cloud	LSZD 423	Drop Head Coupé		
C6528	7504	Silver Cloud	SZD 405	Drop Head Coupé		
C6529	7504	Silver Cloud	LSZD 443	Drop Head Coupé		
C6530	7504	Silver Cloud	SZD 549	Drop Head Coupé		
C6531	7504	Silver Cloud	SZD 475	Drop Head Coupé		
C6532	7504	Silver Cloud	LSZD 493	Drop Head Coupé		
C6533	7504	Silver Cloud	LSZD 519	Drop Head Coupé		
C6534	7504	Silver Cloud	LSZD 539	Drop Head Coupé		
C6535	7504	Silver Cloud	LSAE 9	Drop Head Coupé		
C6537	7504	Silver Cloud	LSAE 19	Drop Head Coupé		
C6538	7504	Silver Cloud	LSAE 53	Drop Head Coupé		
C6539	7504	Silver Cloud	LSAE 67	Drop Head Coupé		
C6540	7504	Silver Cloud	SAE 79	Drop Head Coupé		
C6541	7504	Silver Cloud	LSAE 105	Drop Head Coupé		
C6542	7504	Silver Cloud	LSAE 89	Drop Head Coupé		
C6543	7504	Silver Cloud	SAE 113	Drop Head Coupé		
C6544	7504	Silver Cloud	LSAE 127	Drop Head Coupé		
C6576	7504	Silver Cloud	LSAE 281	Drop Head Coupé		
C6577	7504	Silver Cloud	LSAE 289	Drop Head Coupé		
C6578	7504	Silver Cloud	SAE 293	Drop Head Coupé		
C6579	7504	Silver Cloud	LSAE 347	Drop Head Coupé		
C6580	7504	Silver Cloud	LSAE 497	Drop Head Coupé		
C6581	7504	Silver Cloud	LSAE 499	Drop Head Coupé		
C6582	7504	Silver Cloud	LSAE 561	Drop Head Coupé		
C6583	7504	Silver Cloud	LSAE 583	Drop Head Coupé		
C6585	7504	Silver Cloud	LSAE 639	Drop Head Coupé		

ROLLS-ROYCE "SILVER WRAITH" SEDANCA BY H.J. MULLINER & CO. LTD.

The H. J. Mulliner Sedancas really need a chapter to themselves in order to sort out the different design numbers that have similar or even identical coachwork.

The first post-war design number was 7019, an artists impression of which is illustrated above and which agrees in essence with the coachbuilders drawing. Note that it has a long front wing, merging into the front door and concealing the running board, it also has a double line where the front and rear doors meet at the central pillar.

According to the records, the first body of design No. 7019 was mounted on Silver Wraith, WTA 1 and supplied to the Derby Corporation for use as the Mayor's car. However the photograph of the Mayoral car, seen below, shows it to have shorter front wings and an exposed running board, in fact identical with design No. 7055, illustrated on page 134.

Three photographs of design No. 7042 known as the Mdivani Sedanca de Ville, on the Silver Wraith chassis. Very similar to the artists impression of design No. 7019 but with a single line between the doors.

Above on Silver Wraith, WFC 19 is a Sedanca de Ville, design No. 7055 and below are front and rear photographs of Silver Wraith, WVA 36, a Touring Limousine, design No. 7081, which would appear to be a Limousine version of the upper car.

Three almost identical looking cars, the upper, a Touring Limousine, was prepared for exhibition in America and is similar in design to both the lower cars, but the centre car is Silver Wraith, WYA 87, design No. 7062, in fact a Touring Saloon, exhibited at the Geneva show in 1948 and at present owned by W. B. Carter, Esq. while the lower car is Silver Wraith, WME 44, a Saloon, design No. 7118

H. J. MULLINER

More Sedanca de Villes, the upper cars being of design No. 7120, the centre car is Silver Wraith, WSG 29, while below is a Silver Wraith of design No. 7153.

The above car is somewhat of a mystery. It has obvious affiliations to the lower cars, which are 7 passenger Limousines of design No. 7171, on the Silver Wraith chassis. However the first car of design No. 7171 was delivered in October 1949, whereas the top car was photographed in October 1947. The lower car is Silver Wraith, WFC 25 and was built for the Duchess of Kent.

Phantom IV, 4 AF2, with an Enclosed Drive Limousine body, design No. 7162. This car was delivered in July 1950 to Her Majesty the Queen, when Princess Elizabeth. Note St George and the Dragon on the radiator cap.

Two more pages of Phantom IV's and two cars supplied to H.E. General Franco. Above, an Enclosed Drive Limousine design No. 7181, on chassis No. 4 AF16, delivered in July 1952, and below, delivered in March 1952 is a Cabriolet, design No. 7183 on chassis No. 4 AF18.

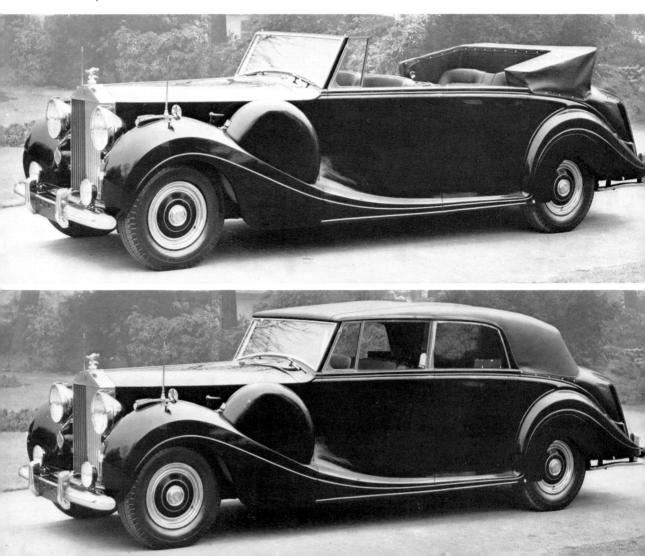

Described as a Cabriolet, but surely a large Drop-head Coupé is this design No. 7205 on Phantom IV, 4 AF 6, supplied to H.M. the Shah of Persia in February 1951. The Saloon on chassis No. 4 AF 8, design No. 7206, was delivered in July 1951 to the Shah of Kuwait.

These Touring Limousines on the Silver Wraith chassis are of design No. 7249, which is an obvious development of design Nos 7062 and 7118, with a higher wing line and a third window on each side.

The rear interior has a bright, neat and uncluttered look.

The only known chassis number of any of these four cars is that of the top car on the opposite page, WVH 68.

It was a car of this design that was exhibited at the Festival of Britain in 1951.

Whilst delving in the H. J. Mulliner records I came across the above car hiding among the Bentley 'R' type Lightweight Saloons. Knowledge of her was denied by all and sundry and it is assumed that she was produced with a batch of Bentleys and given a Silver Dawn radiator and the last Silver Dawn chassis number, that of LSVJ 133 and design No. 7243. The present owner is Arthur Rippey Esq., and the car is exhibited in the Veteran Car Museum in Denver, U.S.A.

The Drop-head Coupé below and on the opposite page is design No. 7296 on Silver Dawn, SHD 50. Two similar bodies were built, this one having what is termed a Jensen rear window.

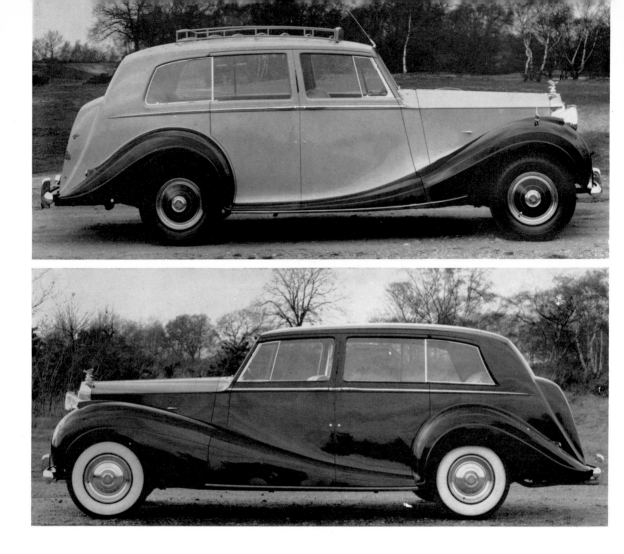

Above, two Enclosed Drive Limousines on the Silver Wraith chassis. The top car is a design No. 7258 and registration No. LXT 20, the lower car is a design No. 7276.
Below, what originally was called an All Metal Sports Limousine and later a Touring Limousine is design No. 7348 on the Silver Wraith chassis.

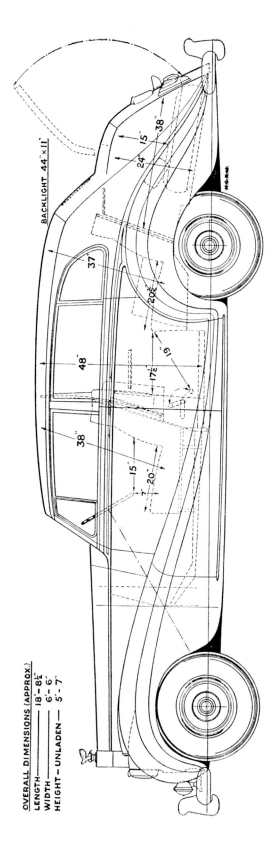

OVERALL DIMENSIONS (APPROX.)

LENGTH	18′ - 8½″
WIDTH	6′ - 6″
HEIGHT — UNLADEN	5′ - 7″

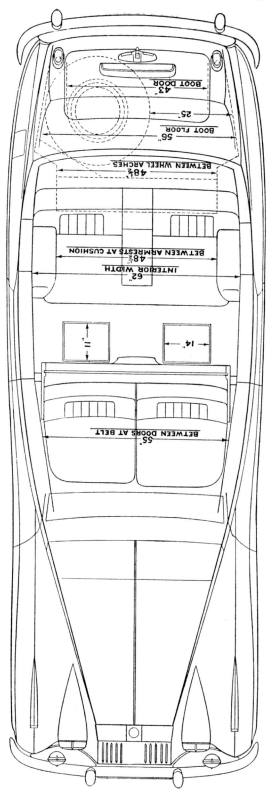

BOOT DOOR 43″

25″

BOOT FLOOR 56″

BETWEEN WHEEL ARCHES 48½″

BETWEEN ARMRESTS AT CUSHION 48½″

INTERIOR WIDTH 62″

BETWEEN DOORS AT BELT 55″

ROLLS-ROYCE SILVER WRAITH TOURING LIMOUSINE   DESIGN 7356

Four photographs of design No. 7356, a Touring Limousine on the long wheelbase Silver Wraith chassis. It appears to be a stretched design No. 7249 and, apart from the size, the easiest form of identification are the non-detachable semi spats on the 7356 rear wings. The bottom car on this page has the revised headlamps introduced in September 1956.

The Maharanee of Baroda's Silver
Wraith, LELW97 with a design
No. 7356 Touring Limousine body.
The two lower photographs illustrate
the car's beautiful interior fittings.

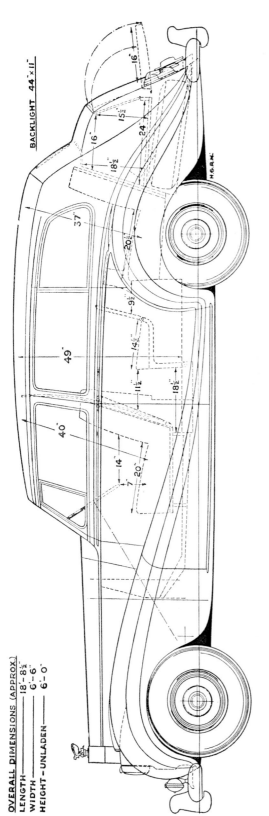

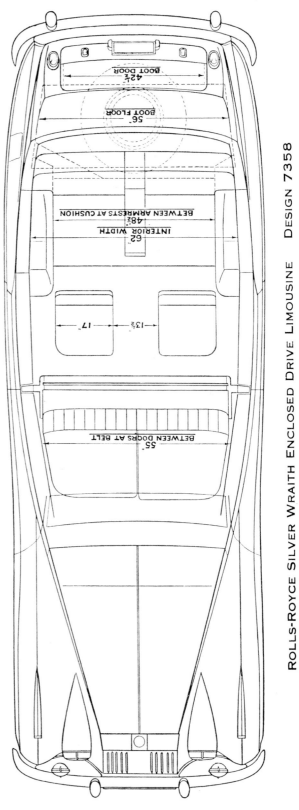

OVERALL DIMENSIONS (APPROX.)

LENGTH ———— 18′-8½″
WIDTH ———— 6′-6″
HEIGHT-UNLADEN ——— 6′-0″

BACKLIGHT 44″×11″

ROLLS-ROYCE SILVER WRAITH ENCLOSED DRIVE LIMOUSINE   DESIGN 7358

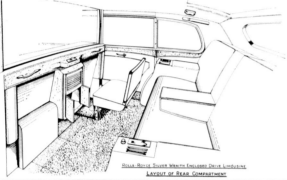

ROLLS-ROYCE SILVER WRAITH ENCLOSED DRIVE LIMOUSINE
LAYOUT OF REAR COMPARTMENT

Two Silver Wraiths with Enclosed Drive Limousine bodies, design No. 7358.

*Phantom IV, 4 BP7, with Enclosed Drive
Limousine coachwork, design No. 7368, built to
the special order of H.R.H. Princess Margaret
and delivered in July 1954.
Note the Spirit of Ecstasy has become equine.*

H. J. MULLINER

Silver Cloud with Drop-head Coupé body, design No. 7410.

Two Drop-head Coupés, above is design No. 7410 and below, design No. 7415, which is a two light version of the upper car. The elimination of the quarter light gives 7415 a heavier look.

Silver Cloud II LLCB16 with a Cabriolet body, design No. 7484, a four door version of design No. 7410 on the long wheelbase chassis. The bottom photograph depicts another car of the same design, although no trace can be found of it in the body book.

The Harold Radford/H. J. Mulliner Estate Car, design No. 7501. After Harold Radford (Coachbuilders) Ltd, had been taken over by H. R. Owen Ltd, H. J. Mulliner produced a few Silver Clouds with Harold Radford designed Estate Car bodies.

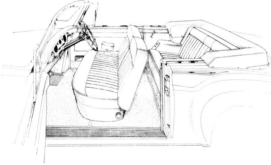

LAYOUT OF INTERIOR WITH HEAD IN FOLDED POSITION

Two photographs and line drawings of the most popular body H. J. Mulliner ever built, design No. 7504. The standard steel Saloon was modified into a two door Drop-head Coupé and mounted on both the Silver Cloud I and II, and by H. J. Mulliner, Park Ward on the Silver Cloud III.

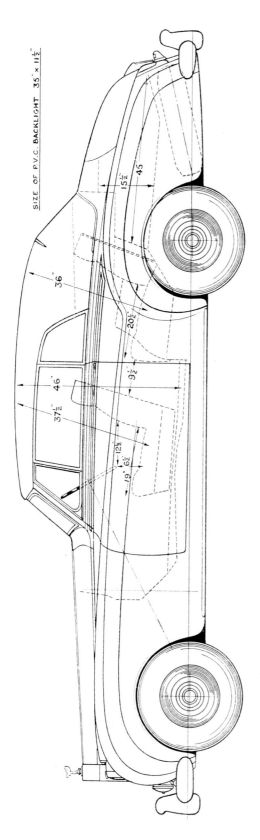

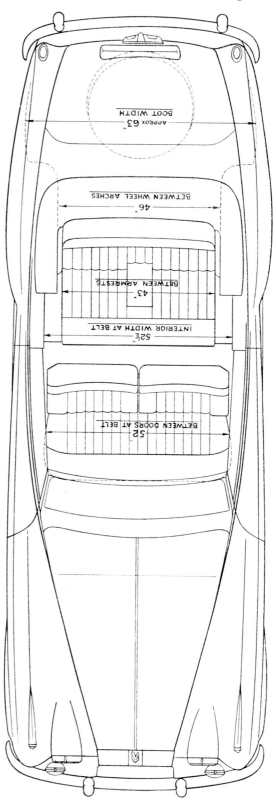

SIZE OF P.V.C. BACKLIGHT 35" × 11½"

The above Limousine is a one car design, No. 7515, on Phantom V, 5 LAS 3 and exhibited on the H. J. Mulliner stand at Earls Court in 1959.
Below is Limousine, design No. 7516, similar to the above car but modified with a certain number of Park Ward, design No. 980, features.

CHAPTER FIVE

PARK WARD

While most of the top names in coachbuilding established themselves in the days of the horse-drawn vehicle, Park Ward was founded at a time when the internal combustion engine was firmly entrenched. W. H. Park and C. W. Ward, both from Sizaire Berwick, founded their business to produce high-class coachwork in 1919. They built their first body on a Rolls-Royce chassis in 1920. Four years later the limited company of Park Ward & Co. was formed, and the premises at High Road, Willesden were extended.

By 1930 ninety per-cent of Park Ward's output was on Rolls-Royce chassis. A closer liaison with Rolls-Royce was established, and a number of experimental bodies were built for the firm.

Park Ward continued to expand and to experiment, and in 1936 they patented the all-steel body framework. Eventually it reached large-scale production for this type of coachwork, as many as eight a week going through the works for mounting on Bentley chassis.

Three years later, in 1939, the firm was purchased by Rolls-Royce Ltd.

After a period of war work Park Ward continued to carry out production and experimental work exclusively for Rolls-Royce Ltd. In 1961 two years after Rolls-Royce Ltd., had acquired H. J. Mulliner Ltd., the company of H. J. Mulliner, Park Ward Ltd., was formed and is now concentrated in the Willesden factory.

Two views of design No. 13, four light Saloons on early Silver Wraith chassis.

Seven seater Touring Limousine design No. 17, on a Silver Wraith chassis. Not a stretched design No. 13, the mudguards are softer in line and the running board is exposed.

This design is not very photogenic and looks much better on the ground than on paper.
Design No. 45, a four door Saloon, again on the early Silver Wraith chassis. Although
owing much of its body and boot design to No. 13, it has a more pleasing wing treatment.

Design No. 51, a Limousine, is really design No. 17 with different mudguarding, the upper photograph has been retouched at sometime giving a false moulding line behind the rear quarter light.

The Wentworth, Park Ward's offering for the 1948 Earls Court Show. The swaging from the top of the front wing to the bottom of the rear wing was added after the body was completed in an attempt to counteract the rather slab sided effect. Design No. 101, only one of which was made.

Four light saloon, design No. 113, softened the hardness of line on the back and boot of designs 13 and 45.

Below: Design No. 146 a six light Limousine similar to design No. 51, but with a more curved roofline.

Design No. 144, a six light
Saloon, upper and lower
photographs being of the 1951
Earls Court Show car. The
centre car competed in the 1950
Monte Carlo Rally and was
awarded the Prix d'honneur in
the Concours de Confort. Turn
back a page to the Wentworth
and note the evolution.

Permutations on the 144 design were numerous, above is design No. 483 another six light saloon, a year later than the top car opposite and below design No. 262 a four light saloon, both on Silver Wraith chassis.

Two examples of the Drop-head Foursome Coupe on the Silver Wraith chassis. Design No. 291, a fine Grand Touring machine in the old meaning of the phrase.

The Silver Dawn edition of the cars on the facing page, design No. 322.

Below: A two door Fixed-Head Coupé design No. 438 on a Silver Dawn chassis.

A 7 seater Limousine design No. 551 on the long wheelbase Silver Wraith chassis, the upper car having unusual rear lights, the lower car is registered PLG 122.

Two interior shots of design No. 551.

Another example of design No. 551 complete with Purdah glass.

One of the few post-war Landaulette bodies, design No. 727 and owing a lot to design No. 551, on a long wheelbase Silver Wraith chassis.

Two light Drop-head Coupe design No. 465 on a Silver Dawn chassis and below also on a Silver Dawn chassis is design No. 555, a four light Drop-head Coupé.

This long wheelbase Silver Wraith, DLW 149 carries a four light Drop-head Foursome Coupé, design No. 571.

Touring Saloon design No. 702, on the Silver Wraith chassis. The above car is on the Park Ward Stand at the 1953 Earls Court Show.

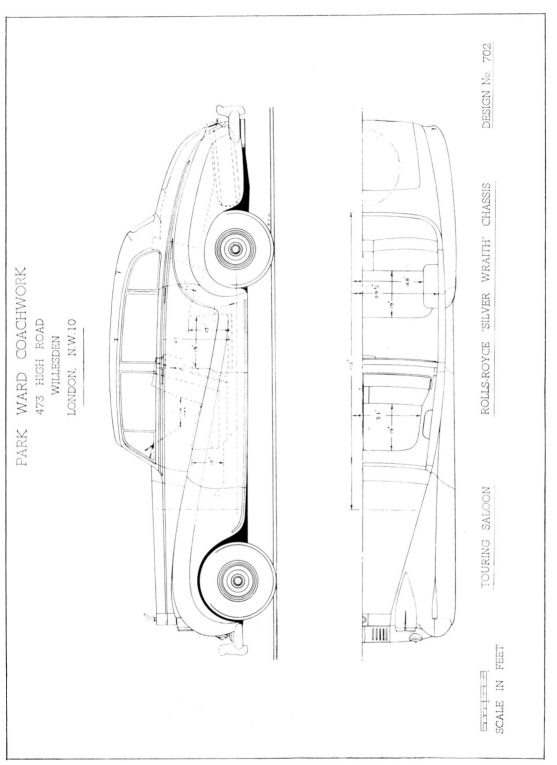

PARK WARD COACHWORK
473 HIGH ROAD
WILLESDEN
LONDON, N.W.10

TOURING SALOON   ROLLS-ROYCE "SILVER WRAITH" CHASSIS   DESIGN No. 702

SCALE IN FEET

Phantom V, 7 passenger Limousine design No. 980, with an overall length of 19' 10".

Her Majesty the Queen Mother's
Phantom V Landaulette
design No. 1104.
As this car was completed after
the merger with H. J. Mulliner,
it is officially of H. J. Mulliner,
Park Ward manufacture, but as
it retained it's Park Ward
design number, I have included it
in this chapter.
H. J. Mulliner, Park Ward
design numbers start at 2000.

"Canberra" Her Majesty The Queen's special 7 passenger Limousine on a Phantom V chassis.

CHAPTER SIX

H. J. MULLINER
PARK WARD

In 1961 the streamlining of resources by Rolls-Royce Ltd., brought about the formation of H. J. Mulliner Park Ward Ltd., from the two coachbuilding companies, H. J. Mulliner Ltd. and Park Ward & Co. Ltd., both then owned by Rolls-Royce.

The two parts of the company continued to operate separately for some time, but with production now being concentrated at the Park Ward Willesden factory. However, in 1968, the repairs and spares departments were transferred to Rolls-Royce at Hythe Road, leaving the factory at Chiswick empty.

At Willesden production of the Limousine on the Phantom VI and the two coupé bodies, fixed and drop head, for the Corniche keep the factory working at full stretch.

Design No. 2003, a direct
descendant of the Park Ward
design No. 980, a seven
passenger Limousine on the
Phantom V chassis.

Design No. 2003/1, really the same Limousine body, this time on a Phantom VI chassis, but now with complete air-conditioning, with separate units for front and rear compartments. The only external difference in design is the air inlet grille on the scuttle, which is missing on the Phantom V.

Hood down, hood up views of design No. 2007, a drop-head Coupé on the Silver Cloud III chassis. This body was a modified standard steel saloon and was deservedly very popular.

A very smooth design for a Drop-head Coupé, No. 2045.

This two door Saloon is the fixed head version of the previous page's Drop-head Coupé and is design No. 2041.

A continuation of the H. J. Mulliner Flying Spur design. This is design No. 2042, a four door six light saloon. The upper car is on Silver Cloud III, SHS 347C.

The Phantom V State Landaulette, design No. 2052, is much closer in line to Park Ward's design No. 980 than to the H.J.M. P.W. design 2003.

The Silver Shadow two door Saloon design No. 3010. As the concept of the standard Silver Shadow was of monocoque construction, entirely new thinking was necessary to evolve this body.

The problems of the two door Saloon were aggravated by the Drop-head Coupé having no roof support. This is design No. 3020.

This Phantom V Landaulette, design No. 2047, supplied to the Ruler of Bahrein, has entirely different rear treatment to the State Landaulette and is more a Landaulette version of design No. 2003.

CHAPTER SEVEN

JAMES YOUNG

James Young, a member of the Institute of British Carriage Makers, acquired the coachbuilding firm of J. K. Hunter, London Road, Bromley in 1863, and rapidly made his mark producing the Bromley Brougham.

It was not until 1908 that the first James Young motor body was built and mounted on a Wolseley chassis for the local Member of Parliament. From then on motor bodies were mounted on a wide variety of chassis until the First World War when the firm switched over to the building of lorries, armoured cars and ambulances.

When the war ended the firm returned to coachbuilding and began exhibiting at the Motor Show in 1925, when they introduced a new style of roof construction to eliminate drumming. Later they designed and patented the parallel opening door which was fitted to bodies on Phantom IIIs, Wraiths and 4¼ litre Bentleys.

In 1937 James Young Ltd., were acquired by Jack Barclay Ltd., and two years later switched again to war work on the outbreak of the Second World War. The factory was burnt out in the 1941 blitz, rebuilt, only to be badly damaged by a flying bomb.

Coachwork for Rolls-Royce and Bentley cars was immediately resumed at the end of hostilities with an annual output of about sixty bodies. However, with the advent of the chassisless Rolls-Royce Silver Shadow and Bentley T type, fifty modifications to the standard Rolls-Royce body were made before coachbuilding was finally ended in 1967.

James Young, now part of the Dutton-Forshaw group, concentrate on repairs and maintenance of coachwork and as a sales organisation of Fiat cars.

Extracts from
James Young body book
referring to coachwork
mounted on Rolls-Royce
chassis only

JAMES YOUNG

JOB NO	DESIGN NO	CHASSIS	CHASSIS NO	TYPE OF BODY	REMARKS
1600	WR 16	Silver Wraith		Saloon Coupé	
1601	WR 16	Silver Wraith		Saloon Coupé	
1602	WR 16	Silver Wraith		Saloon Coupé	
1700	WR 17	Silver Wraith		4 door Sports Saloon	
1701	WR 17	Silver Wraith		4 door Sports Saloon	
1702	WR 17	Silver Wraith		4 door Sports Saloon	
1703	WR 17	Silver Wraith		4 door Sports Saloon	
1704	WR 17	Silver Wraith		4 door Sports Saloon	
1705	WR 17	Silver Wraith		4 door Sports Saloon	
1706	WR 17	Silver Wraith		4 door Sports Saloon	
1707	WR 17	Silver Wraith		4 door Sports Saloon	
1708	WR 17	Silver Wraith		4 door Sports Saloon	
1709	WR 17	Silver Wraith		4 door Sports Saloon	
1710	WR 17	Silver Wraith		4 door Sports Saloon	
1711	WR 17	Silver Wraith		4 door Sports Saloon	
1712	WR 17	Silver Wraith		4 door Sports Saloon	
1713	WR 17	Silver Wraith		4 door Sports Saloon	
1714	WR 17	Silver Wraith		4 door Sports Saloon	
1715	WR 17	Silver Wraith		4 door Sports Saloon	
1716	WR 17	Silver Wraith		4 door Sports Saloon	
1717	WR 17	Silver Wraith		4 door Sports Saloon	
1718	WR 17	Silver Wraith		4 door Sports Saloon	
1719	WR 17	Silver Wraith		4 door Sports Saloon	
1721	WR 17	Silver Wraith		4 door Sports Saloon	
1722	WR 17	Silver Wraith		4 door Sports Saloon	
1723	WR 17	Silver Wraith		4 door Sports Saloon	
1724	WR 17	Silver Wraith		4 door Sports Saloon	
1725	*	Silver Wraith		4 door Saloon	
1726	*	Silver Wraith		4 door Saloon	
1727	*	Silver Wraith		4 door Saloon	
1728	*	Silver Wraith		4 door Saloon	
1729	*	Silver Wraith		4 door Saloon	
1730	*	Silver Wraith		4 door Saloon	
1731	*	Silver Wraith		4 door Saloon	
1732	*	Silver Wraith		4 door Saloon	
1733	*	Silver Wraith		4 door Saloon	
1735	*	Silver Wraith		4 door Saloon	
1736	*	Silver Wraith		4 door Saloon	
1737	*	Silver Wraith		4 door Saloon	
1738	*	Silver Wraith		4 door Saloon	
1739	*	Silver Wraith		4 door Saloon	
1742	*	Silver Wraith		4 door Saloon	
1743	*	Silver Wraith		4 door Saloon	
1746	*	Silver Wraith		4 door Saloon	
1747	*	Silver Wraith		4 door Saloon	
1748	*	Silver Wraith		4 door Saloon	
1749	*	Silver Wraith	WHD 16	4 door Saloon	
1750	*	Silver Wraith	WHD 29	4 door Saloon	
1751	*	Silver Wraith	WHD 25	4 door Saloon	
1752	*	Silver Wraith	WHD 94	4 door Saloon	
1753	*	Silver Wraith	WHD 20	4 door Saloon	
1754	*	Silver Wraith	WLE 1	4 door Saloon	

*WR 17 or WR 18. No individual identification

JOB NO	DESIGN NO	CHASSIS	CHASSIS NO	TYPE OF BODY	REMARKS
1755	*	Silver Wraith	WLE 6	4 door Saloon	
1756	*	Silver Wraith	WME 9	4 door Saloon	
1757	*	Silver Wraith	WME 18	4 door Saloon	
1760	WR 25	Silver Wraith		4 door Sports Saloon	
1761	WR 25	Silver Wraith	WHD 82	4 door Sports Saloon	
1762	WR 25	Silver Wraith	WHD 96	4 door Sports Saloon	
1763	WR 25	Silver Wraith	WHD 90	4 door Sports Saloon	
1764	WR 25	Silver Wraith	WME 76	4 door Sports Saloon	
1765	WR 25	Silver Wraith	WME 47	4 door Sports Saloon	
1766	WR 25	Silver Wraith	WME 51	4 door Sports Saloon	
1767	WR 25	Silver Wraith	WME 92	4 door Sports Saloon	
1768	WR 25	Silver Wraith	WME 91	4 door Sports Saloon	
1769	WR 25	Silver Wraith	WOF 42	4 door Sports Saloon	
1770	WR 25	Silver Wraith	WOF 45	4 door Sports Saloon	
1771	WR 25	Silver Wraith	WOF 10	4 door Sports Saloon	
1772	WR 25	Silver Wraith	WOF 23	4 door Sports Saloon	
1773	WR 25	Silver Wraith	WOF 38	4 door Sports Saloon	
1774	WR 25	Silver Wraith	WSG 24	4 door Sports Saloon	
1775	WR 25	Silver Wraith	WOF 67	4 door Sports Saloon	
1776	WR 25	Silver Wraith	LWSG 47	4 door Sports Saloon	
1777	WR 25	Silver Wraith	WOF 60	4 door Sports Saloon	
1778	WR 25	Silver Wraith	WSG 1	4 door Sports Saloon	
1779	WR 25	Silver Wraith	WOF 75	4 door Sports Saloon	
1780	WR 25	Silver Wraith	LWSG 54	4 door Sports Saloon	
1781	WR 25	Silver Wraith	WSG 19	4 door Sports Saloon	
1782	WR 25	Silver Wraith	WSG 46	4 door Sports Saloon	
1783	WR 25	Silver Wraith	WSG 44	4 door Sports Saloon	
1784	WR 25	Silver Wraith	WSG 28	4 door Sports Saloon	
1785	WR 25	Silver Wraith	LWME 33	4 door Sports Saloon	
1786	WR 25	Silver Wraith	WSG 71	4 door Sports Saloon	
1787	WR 26	Silver Wraith	WVH 8	4 door Saloon	
1788	WR 26	Silver Wraith	WVH 21	4 door Saloon	
1789	WR 26	Silver Wraith	WVH 38	4 door Saloon	
1790	WR 26	Silver Wraith	WVH 19	4 door Saloon	
1791	WR 26	Silver Wraith	WVH 26	4 door Saloon	
1792	WR 26	Silver Wraith	WVH 25	4 door Saloon	
1793	WR 27	Silver Wraith	LWVH 41	Sedanca de Ville	
1794	WR 26	Silver Wraith	WVH 48	4 door Saloon	
1795	WR 26	Silver Wraith	WVH 54	4 door Saloon	
1796	WR 26	Silver Wraith	WVH 30	4 door Saloon	
1797	WR 26	Silver Wraith	WVH 23	4 door Saloon	
1798	WR 26	Silver Wraith	WVH 72	4 door Saloon	
1810	WRM 30	Silver Wraith	BLW 43	4 door Saloon	Paris Salon 1953
1811	WRM 30	Silver Wraith	BLW 63	4 door Saloon	Earls Court Show 1953
1812	WRM 30	Silver Wraith	BLW 64	4 door Saloon	
1813	WRM 30	Silver Wraith	BLW 65	4 door Saloon	
1814	WRM 30	Silver Wraith	CLW 8	4 door Saloon	Geneva Show 1954
1815	WRM 30	Silver Wraith	CLW 18	4 door Saloon	
1816	WRM 30	Silver Wraith	CLW 21	4 door Saloon	
1817	WRM 30	Silver Wraith	CLW 19	4 door Saloon	
1818	WRM 30	Silver Wraith	DLW 33	4 door Saloon	
1819	WRM 30	Silver Wraith	LCLW 4	4 door Saloon	New boot line

*WR 17 or WR 18. No individual identification

JAMES YOUNG

JOB NO	DESIGN NO	CHASSIS	CHASSIS NO	TYPE OF BODY	REMARKS
1820	WRM 30	Silver Wraith	CLW 20	4 door Saloon	
1821	WRM 30	Silver Wraith	DLW 74	4 door Saloon	
1822	WRM 30	Silver Wraith	DLW 75	4 door Saloon	
1823	WRM 30	Silver Wraith	DLW 125	4 door Saloon	
1824	WRM 30	Silver Wraith	DLW 26	4 door Saloon	
1825	WRM 30	Silver Wraith	DLW 27	4 door Saloon	Roof raised
1826	WRM 30	Silver Wraith	DLW 76	4 door Saloon	
1827	WRM 31	Silver Wraith	DLW 41	4 door Saloon	Revised wings. Paris Salon 1954
1828	WRM 30	Silver Wraith	DLW 49	4 door Saloon	Earls Court Show 1954
1829	WRM 30	Silver Wraith	DLW 53	4 door Saloon	
1830	WRM 30	Silver Wraith	DLW 104	4 door Saloon	
1831	WRM 30	Silver Wraith	DLW 108	4 door Saloon	
1832	WRM 30	Silver Wraith	DLW 112	4 door Saloon	
1833	WRM 30	Silver Wraith	DLW 111	4 door Saloon	
1834	WRM 30	Silver Wraith	DLW 128	4 door Saloon	
1835	WRM 30	Silver Wraith	DLW 146	4 door Saloon	
1836	WRM 27	Silver Wraith	LDLW 105	Sedanca de Ville	
1837	SW10	Silver Wraith	LDLW 115	4 door Saloon	Special boot
1838	WRM 30	Silver Wraith	DLW 117	4 door Saloon	Geneva Show 1955
1839	WRM 30	Silver Wraith	LDLW 119	4 door Saloon	
1840	WRM 30	Silver Wraith	DLW 120	4 door Saloon	
1841	WRM 31	Silver Wraith	DLW 147	4 door Saloon	
1842	WRM 31	Silver Wraith	DLW 153	4 door Saloon	
1843	WRM 31	Silver Wraith	DLW 156	4 door Saloon	
1844	WRM 31	Silver Wraith	DLW 169	4 door Saloon	
1845	WRM 31	Silver Wraith	DLW 171	4 door Saloon	
1846	WRM 31	Silver Wraith	DLW 167	4 door Saloon	
1847	WRM 31	Silver Wraith	ELW 12	4 door Saloon	
1848	WRM 31	Silver Wraith	LELW 1	4 door Saloon	Paris Salon 1955
1849	WRM 31	Silver Wraith	ELW 7	4 door Saloon	Earls Court Show 1955
1850	WRM 31	Silver Wraith	ELW 23	4 door Saloon	
1851	WRM 31	Silver Wraith	ELW 46	4 door Saloon	
1852	WRM 31	Silver Wraith	ELW 37	4 door Saloon	
1853	WRM 31	Silver Wraith	ELW 68	4 door Saloon	
1854	WRM 31	Silver Wraith	LELW 86	4 door Saloon	New York Show 1956
1855	WRM 31	Silver Wraith	ELW 52	4 door Saloon	
1856	WRM 31	Silver Wraith	LELW 71	4 door Saloon	
1857	WRM 31	Silver Wraith	ELW 93	4 door Saloon	Paris Salon 1956
1858	WRM 31	Silver Wraith	FLW 1	4 door Saloon	
1859	WRM 31	Silver Wraith	FLW 2	4 door Saloon	
1860	WRM 31	Silver Wraith	ELW 32	4 door Saloon	
1861	WRM 31	Silver Wraith	LELW 59	4 door Saloon	
1862	WRM 31	Silver Wraith	LELW 25	4 door Saloon	
1863	WRM 31	Silver Wraith	FLW 12	4 door Saloon	Earls Court Show 1956
1864	WRM 27	Silver Wraith	ELW 44	Sedanca de Ville	Geneva Show 1956
1865	WRM 31	Silver Wraith	ELW 54	4 door Saloon	
1866	WRM 27	Silver Wraith	LELW 72	Sedanca de Ville	
1867	WRM 35S	Silver Wraith	LELW 39	7 seater Limousine	
1868	WRM 35S	Silver Wraith	LELW 80	7 seater Limousine	
1869	WRM 35S	Silver Wraith	FLW 14	7 seater Limousine	Earls Court Show 1956
1870	SW 10	Silver Wraith	LELW 43	4 door Saloon	Special boot
1871	WRM 31	Silver Wraith	FLW 32	4 door Saloon	

JAMES YOUNG

JOB NO	DESIGN NO	CHASSIS	CHASSIS NO	TYPE OF BODY	REMARKS
1872	WRM 31	Silver Wraith	LELW 91	4 door Saloon	
1873	SW 10	Silver Wraith	LELW 88	4 door Saloon	Special boot
1874	WRM 31	Silver Wraith	FLW 36	4 door Saloon	
1875	WRM 31	Silver Wraith	LELW 95	4 door Saloon	
1876	WRM 31	Silver Wraith	FLW 38	4 door Saloon	
1877	WRM 31	Silver Wraith	FLW 51	4 door Saloon	
1878	WRM 31	Silver Wraith	FLW 42	4 door Saloon	
1879	WRM 31	Silver Wraith	FLW 40	4 door Saloon	
1880	WRM 35S	Silver Wraith	LELW 80	7 seater Limousine	
1881	WRM 35S	Silver Wraith	FLW 56	7 seater Limousine	Geneva Show 1957
1882	WRM 35S	Silver Wraith	LFLW 80	7 seater Limousine	
1883	WRM 31	Silver Wraith	FLW 74	4 door Saloon	Geneva Show 1957
1884	WRM 31	Silver Wraith	LFLW 89	4 door Saloon	
1885	WRM 31S	Silver Wraith	FLW 73		
1886	WRM 31	Silver Wraith	LFLW 91	4 door Saloon	
1887	WRM 31	Silver Wraith	LFLW 96	4 door Saloon	
1888	WRM 31	Silver Wraith	FLW 53	4 door Saloon	
1889	WRM 12	Silver Wraith	LFLW 59	2 door Saloon	
1890	WRM 35S	Silver Wraith	FLW 85	7 seater Limousine	
1891	WRM 31	Silver Wraith	FLW 82	4 door Saloon	Earls Court Show 1957
1892	WRM 35S	Silver Wraith	FLW 55	7 seater Limousine	
1893	WRM 35S	Silver Wraith	LGLW 6	7 seater Limousine	
1894	WRM 31	Silver Wraith	GLW 19	4 door Saloon	
1895	WRM 31	Silver Wraith	GLW 16	4 door Saloon	Full width division. Geneva Show 1958
1896	WRM 31	Silver Wraith	GLW 21	4 door Saloon	
1897	WRM 31	Silver Wraith	HLW 1	4 door Saloon	
1898	WRM 35S	Silver Wraith	LGLW 10	7 seater Limousine	New York Show 1958
1899	WRM 35S	Silver Wraith	LHLW 14	7 seater Limousine	
9000	WRM 35S	Silver Wraith	LGLW 18	7 seater Limousine	
9001	WRM 31	Silver Wraith	HLW 2	4 door Saloon	Revised boot lid. Paris Salon 1958
9002	WRM 31	Silver Wraith	HLW 30	4 door Saloon	Revised boot lid
9003	WR 50	Silver Wraith	LHLW 3	4 door Saloon	Special
9004	WRM 31	Silver Wraith	HLW 34	4 door Saloon	Revised boot lid
9005	WRM 35S	Silver Wraith	HLW 33	7 seater Limousine	
9006	SW 10	Silver Wraith	LHLW 28	4 door Saloon	
9007	WRM 31	Silver Wraith	LHLW 29	4 door Saloon	
9008	WRM 35S	Silver Wraith	LHLW 43	7 seater Limousine	
9009	WRM 35S	Silver Wraith	LHLW 39	7 seater Limousine	
2000	WR 20	Silver Wraith		Drop Head Coupé	
2001	WR 20	Silver Wraith		Drop Head Coupé	
2002	WR 20	Silver Wraith		Drop Head Coupé	Made at Gurney Nutting
2003	WR 20	Silver Wraith		Drop Head Coupé	Made at Gurney Nutting
2004	WR 20	Silver Wraith		Drop Head Coupé	
2005	WR 20	Silver Wraith		Drop Head Coupé	Made at Gurney Nutting
2006	WR 20	Silver Wraith		Drop Head Coupé	Made at Gurney Nutting
2007	WR 20	Silver Wraith		Drop Head Coupé	Made at Gurney Nutting
2008	WR 20	Silver Wraith		Drop Head Coupé	Made at Gurney Nutting
2009	WR 20	Silver Wraith		Drop Head Coupé	
2010	WR 20	Silver Wraith		Drop Head Coupé	Made at Gurney Nutting
2011	WR 20	Silver Wraith		Drop Head Coupé	Made at Gurney Nutting
2020	WR 19	Silver Wraith	WME 69	4 door Sports Saloon	
2021	WR 19	Silver Wraith	WOF 66	4 door Sports Saloon	

JOB NO	DESIGN NO	CHASSIS	CHASSIS NO	TYPE OF BODY	REMARKS
2022	WR 19	Silver Wraith		4 door Sports Saloon	
2023	WR 19	Silver Wraith	WVH 7	4 door Sports Saloon	
2024	WR 19	Silver Wraith	WVH 29	4 door Sports Saloon	
2025	WR 19	Silver Wraith	WVH 99	4 door Sports Saloon	
2026	WR 19	Silver Wraith	WVH 66	4 door Sports Saloon	
2212	C 20 SD	Silver Dawn	SNF 27	4 door Saloon	
2223	C 20 SD	Silver Dawn	SOG 100	4 door Saloon	
2224	C 20 SDB	Silver Dawn	SOG 42	4 door Saloon	
2229	C 20 SD	Silver Dawn	SOG 44	4 door Saloon	
2233	C 20 ASD	Silver Dawn	SPG 101	4 door Saloon	
2238	C 20 SD	Silver Dawn	SRH 50	4 door Saloon	
2239	C 20 SD	Silver Dawn	STH 95	4 door Saloon	
2240	C 20 SD	Silver Dawn	SRH 68	4 door Saloon	
2241	C 20 SD	Silver Dawn	SRH 70	4 door Saloon	
2242	C 20 SD	Silver Dawn	STH 57	4 door Saloon	
2243	C 20 SD	Silver Dawn	STH 97	4 door Saloon	
4000	SC 10	Silver Cloud	SWA 54	4 door Saloon	Paris Salon 1955
4001	SC 10	Silver Cloud	SWA 52	4 door Saloon	Earls Court Show 1955
4002	SC 10	Silver Cloud	SWA 50	4 door Saloon	
4003	SC 10	Silver Cloud	SWA 60	4 door Saloon	
3018	SC 10	Silver Cloud	SWA 90	4 door Saloon	
4005	SC 10	Silver Cloud	SWA 65	4 door Saloon	
4006	SC 10	Silver Cloud	SWA 88	4 door Saloon	
4007	SC 10	Silver Cloud	SWA 110	4 door Saloon	
4008	SC 10	Silver Cloud	SXA 47	4 door Saloon	
4009	SC 10	Silver Cloud	SWA 96	4 door Saloon	
4010	SC 10S	Silver Cloud	SXA 129	4 door Saloon	large backlight
4011	SC 10	Silver Cloud	SZB 43	4 door Saloon	
4012	SC 10	Silver Cloud	SXA 121	4 door Saloon	
4013	SC 10	Silver Cloud	SXA 119	4 door Saloon	
4014	SC 10	Silver Cloud	SXA 133	4 door Saloon	
4015	SC 10	Silver Cloud	LSXA 137	4 door Saloon	
4016	SC 10	Silver Cloud	LSYB 114	4 door Saloon	Paris Salon 1956
4017	SC 10	Silver Cloud	SZB 41	4 door Saloon	Earls Court Show 1956
4018	SC 10	Silver Cloud	LSBC 98	4 door Saloon	
4019	SC 10	Silver Cloud	SXA 135	4 door Saloon	
4020	SC 10	Silver Cloud	SZB 205	4 door Saloon	
4021	SC 10	Silver Cloud	SDD 306	4 door Saloon	
4022	SC 10	Silver Cloud	SDD 308	4 door Saloon	
4023	SC 10	Silver Cloud	SDD 310	4 door Saloon	
4024	SC 10	Silver Cloud	SGE 248	4 door Saloon	
4025	SC 20	Silver Cloud	LSDD 44	2 door Saloon	
4026	SC 20	Silver Cloud	LSFE 99	2 door Sedanca Coupé	
4028	SC 10	Silver Cloud	SZB 203	4 door Saloon	
4029	SC 20	Silver Cloud	LSGE 448	2 door Drop Head Coupé	
4030	SC 20	Silver Cloud	LSHF 111	2 door Saloon Coupé	High wing
4031	SC 20	Silver Cloud	LSHF 169	2 door Drop Head Coupé	
4032	SC 20	Silver Cloud	LSJF 112	2 door Sedanca Coupé	
4033	SC 20	Silver Cloud	LSJF 202	2 seat Drop Head Coupé	
4050	SC 12	Silver Cloud	ALC 2	4 door, 6 light Saloon	Earls Court Show 1957
4051	SC 12	Silver Cloud	ALC 3	4 door, 6 light Saloon	Paris Salon 1957
4052	SC 12	Silver Cloud	ALC 7	4 door, 6 light Saloon	

JOB NO	DESIGN NO	CHASSIS	CHASSIS NO	TYPE OF BODY	REMARKS
4053	SC 12	Silver Cloud	ALC 8	4 door, 6 light Saloon	
4054	SC 12	Silver Cloud	ALC 6	4 door, 6 light Saloon	
4055	SC 12	Silver Cloud	ALC 4	4 door, 6 light Saloon	
4056	SC 12	Silver Cloud	ALC 20	4 door, 6 light Saloon	Geneva Show 1958
4057	SC 12	Silver Cloud	LALC 26	4 door, 6 light Saloon	
4058	SC 12	Silver Cloud	ALC 22	4 door, 6 light Saloon	
4059	SC 12	Silver Cloud	ALC 23	4 door, 6 light Saloon	
4060	SC 12	Silver Cloud	BLC 15	4 door, 6 light Saloon	Earls Court Show 1958
4061	SC 12	Silver Cloud	BLC 14	4 door, 6 light Saloon	
4062	SC 12	Silver Cloud	BLC 44	4 door, 6 light Saloon	
4063	SC 12	Silver Cloud	LCLC 6	4 door, 6 light Saloon	New York Show 1959
4064	SC 12	Silver Cloud	CLC 14	4 door, 6 light Saloon	Geneva Show 1959
4065	SC 12	Silver Cloud	CLC 7	4 door, 6 light Saloon	
4066	SC 12	Silver Cloud	LCLC 4	4 door, 6 light Saloon	
4100	SCT 12	Silver Cloud II	LCA 2	4 door, 6 light Saloon	Earls Court Show 1959
4101	SCT 12	Silver Cloud II	LCA 3	4 door, 6 light Saloon	
4102	SCT 12	Silver Cloud II	LLCA 4	4 door, 6 light Saloon	
4104	SCT 12	Silver Cloud II	LCA 23	4 door, 6 light Saloon	
4105	SCT 12	Silver Cloud II	LCA 26	4 door, 6 light Saloon	
4106	SCT 12	Silver Cloud II	LCA 25	4 door, 6 light Saloon	
4107	SCT 12	Silver Cloud II	LCA 27	4 door, 6 light Saloon	
4108	SCT 12	Silver Cloud II	LLCA 43	4 door, 6 light Saloon	
4109	SCT 12	Silver Cloud II	LLCA 38	4 door, 6 light Saloon	Special quarter and division
4110	SCT 100	Silver Cloud II	LCB 7	Touring Limousine	E.C. Show, 1960, Low roof line
4111	SCT 100	Silver Cloud II	LCB 6	Touring Limousine	High roof line
4112	SCT 100	Silver Cloud II	LCB 8	Touring Limousine	Low roof line
4113	SCT 100	Silver Cloud II	LCB 24	Touring Limousine	High roof line
4114	SCT 100	Silver Cloud II	LCB 25	Touring Limousine	
4115	SCT 100	Silver Cloud II	LCB 68	Touring Limousine	
4116	SCT 100	Silver Cloud II	LCB 38	Touring Limousine	
4120	SCT 100	Silver Cloud II	LCB 81	Touring Limousine	
4121	SCT 100	Silver Cloud II	LCB 69	Touring Limousine	
4122	SCT 100	Silver Cloud II	LCB 39	Touring Limousine	
4123	SCT 100	Silver Cloud II	LLCC 2	Touring Limousine	
4124	SCT 100	Silver Cloud II	LCB 101	Touring Limousine	4 light
4125	SCT 100	Silver Cloud II	LLCC 3	Touring Limousine	
4126	SCT 100	Silver Cloud II	LCC 39	Touring Limousine	
4127	SCT 100	Silver Cloud II	LCC 8	Touring Limousine	Earls Court Show 1961
4128	SCT 100	Silver Cloud II	LCC 23	Touring Limousine	
4129	SCT 100	Silver Cloud II	LCC 68	Touring Limousine	
4130	SCT 100	Silver Cloud II	LCC 40	Touring Limousine	
4131	SCT 100	Silver Cloud II	LCC 47	Touring Limousine	
4132	SCT 100	Silver Cloud II	LCC 46	Touring Limousine	
4134	SCT 100	Silver Cloud II	LLCC 65	Touring Limousine	
4135	SCT 100	Silver Cloud II	LCC 66	Touring Limousine	
4136	SCT 100	Silver Cloud II	LCC 45	Touring Limousine	
4137	SCT 100	Silver Cloud II	LCC 76	Touring Limousine	
4138	SCT 100	Silver Cloud II	LCC 101	Touring Limousine	
4139	SCT 100	Silver Cloud II	LCD 1	Touring Limousine	
4140	SCT 100	Silver Cloud II	LCD 19	Touring Limousine	
4141	SCT 100	Silver Cloud III	CAL 3	Touring Limousine	Earls Court Show 1962
4142	SCT 100	Silver Cloud III	CAL 49	Touring Limousine	

JOB NO	DESIGN NO	CHASSIS	CHASSIS NO	TYPE OF BODY	REMARKS
4143	SCT 100	Silver Cloud III	CAL 5	Touring Limousine	
4144	SCT 100	Silver Cloud III	LCAL 1	Touring Limousine	Paris Salon 1962
4145	SCT 100	Silver Cloud III	LCAL 17	Touring Limousine	
4146	SCT 100	Silver Cloud III	CAL 55	Touring Limousine	
4147	SCT 100	Silver Cloud III	CAL 57	Touring Limousine	
4149	SCT 100	Silver Cloud III	CAL 83	Touring Limousine	
4150	SCT 100	Silver Cloud III	CBL 15	Touring Limousine	
4151	SCT 100	Silver Cloud III	CBL 31	Touring Limousine	
4152	SCT 100	Silver Cloud III	CBL 17	Touring Limousine	
4153	SCT 100	Silver Cloud III	CBL 29	Touring Limousine	
4154	SCT 100	Silver Cloud III	CBL 57	Touring Limousine	
4155	SCT 100	Silver Cloud III	CBL 51	Touring Limousine	
4156	SCT 100	Silver Cloud III	LCCL 1	Touring Limousine	
4157	SCT 100	Silver Cloud III	CCL 5	Touring Limousine	
4158	SCT 100	Silver Cloud III	CCL 17	Touring Limousine	
4159	SCT 100	Silver Cloud III	CCL 33	Touring Limousine	
4160	SCT 100	Silver Cloud III	CCL 27	Touring Limousine	Earls Court Show 1963
4161	SCT 100	Silver Cloud III	CCL 35	Touring Limousine	
4162	SCT 100	Silver Cloud III	CCL 47	Touring Limousine	
4163	SCT 100	Silver Cloud III	CCL 57	Touring Limousine	
4164	SCT 100	Silver Cloud III	CCL 61	Touring Limousine	
4165	SCT 100	Silver Cloud III	CCL 73	Touring Limousine	
4166	SCT 100	Silver Cloud III	CCL 69	Touring Limousine	
4168	SCT 200	Silver Cloud III	LCDL 1	Touring Limousine	2 door
4169	SCT 100	Silver Cloud III	LCDL 15	Touring Limousine	
4170	SCT 100	Silver Cloud III	CCL 83	Touring Limousine	
4171	SCT 100	Silver Cloud III	CDL 53	Touring Limousine	
4172	SCT 100	Silver Cloud III	CCL 97	Touring Limousine	
4173	SCT 100	Silver Cloud III	CDL 79	Touring Limousine	
4175	SCT 100	Silver Cloud III	LCDL 81	Touring Limousine	Paris Salon 1964
4176	SCT 100	Silver Cloud III	CEL 11	Touring Limousine	
4177	SCT 200	Silver Cloud III	CEL 19	Touring Limousine	2 door, Special quarter lights
4178	SCT 100	Silver Cloud III	CEL 41	Touring Limousine	
4179	SCT 100	Silver Cloud III	CEL 47	Touring Limousine	
4180	SCT 100	Silver Cloud III	LCEL 59	Touring Limousine	
4181	SCT 100	Silver Cloud III	CEL 71	Touring Limousine	
4184	SCT 100	Silver Cloud III	CEL 101	Touring Limousine	
4185	SCT 100	Silver Cloud III	CFL 3	Touring Limousine	
4186	SCT 100	Silver Cloud III	CFL 15	Touring Limousine	
4188	SC 179	Silver Cloud III	LCFL 39	Touring Limousine	Special quarter lights
5246	SCV 100	Silver Cloud III	SEV 121	4 door, 6 light Saloon	Earls Court Show 1963
5248	SCV 100	Silver Cloud III	SFU 81	4 door, 6 light Saloon	Geneva Show 1964
5250	SCV 100	Silver Cloud III	SFU 127	4 door, 6 light Saloon	
5251	SCV 100	Silver Cloud III	SFU 365	4 door, 6 light Saloon	
5252	SCV 100	Silver Cloud III	SFU 411	4 door, 6 light Saloon	
5253	SCV 100	Silver Cloud III	LSFU 651	4 door, 6 light Saloon	
5254	SCV 100	Silver Cloud III	SFU 619	4 door, 6 light Saloon	
5255	SCV 100	Silver Cloud III	SFU 513	4 door, 6 light Saloon	
5256	SCV 100	Silver Cloud III	SGT 567	4 door, 6 light Saloon	
5257	SCV 100	Silver Cloud III	SGT 609C	2 door, 4 light Saloon	Earls Court Show 1964
5258	SCV 100	Silver Cloud III	LSGT 607C	2 door, 4 light Saloon	
5259	SCV 100	Silver Cloud III	LSGT 635C	4 door, 6 light Saloon	

JOB NO	DESIGN NO	CHASSIS	CHASSIS NO.	TYPE OF BODY	REMARKS
5260	SCV 100	Silver Cloud III	SHS 343C	4 door, 6 light Saloon	
5261	SCV 100	Silver Cloud III	SHS 305C	4 door, 6 light Saloon	
5262	SCV 100	Silver Cloud III	SHS 313C	4 door, 6 light Saloon	
5264	SCV 100	Silver Cloud III	SJR 569C	4 door, 6 light Saloon	
5266	SCV 100	Silver Cloud III	SJR 589C	4 door, 6 light Saloon	
5269	SCV 100	Silver Cloud III	SJR 621C	4 door, 6 light Saloon	
5271	SCV 100	Silver Cloud III	CSC 17B	4 door, 6 light Saloon	
5272	SCV 100	Silver Cloud III	CSC 31B	2 door, 4 light Saloon	
5276	SCV 100	Silver Cloud III	CSC 91B	2 door, 4 light Saloon	
5277	SCV 100	Silver Cloud III	CSC 103B	4 door, 6 light Saloon	
5278	SCV 100	Silver Cloud III	CSC 101B	2 door, 4 light Saloon	
5279	SCV 100	Silver Cloud III	CSC 117B	4 door, 6 light Saloon	
5280	SCV 100	Silver Cloud III	CSC 115B	4 door, 6 light Saloon	
5281	SCV 100	Silver Cloud III	LCSC 99B	2 door, 4 light Saloon	
9015	PV 15	Phantom V	5 AS 17	7 passenger Limousine	
9016	PV 10M	Phantom V	5 AT 48	7 passenger Limousine	Special boot and roof
9017	PV 15	Phantom V	5 AS 23	7 passenger Limousine	
9018	PV 15	Phantom V	5 LAS 73	7 passenger Limousine	New York Show 1960
9019	PV 15	Phantom V	5 AT 30	7 passenger Limousine	Special backlight
9020	PV 15	Phantom V	5 LAS 59	7 passenger Limousine	Special quarter light
9021	PV 15	Phantom V	5 LAT 88	7 passenger Limousine	Earls Court Show 1960
9022	PV 15	Phantom V	5 AT 74	7 passenger Limousine	
9023	PV 15	Phantom V	5 BV 9	7 passenger Limousine	
9024	PV 15	Phantom V	5 BV 1	7 passenger Limousine	
9026	PV 15	Phantom V	5 LBV 47	7 passenger Limousine	New York Show 1961
9027	PV 15	Phantom V	5 LAT 98	7 passenger Limousine	
9028	PV 15	Phantom V	5 BV 87	7 passenger Limousine	
9029	PV 15	Phantom V	5 BX 12	7 passenger Limousine	
9030	PV 15	Phantom V	5 LBX 70	7 passenger Limousine	Earls Court Show 1961
9031	PV 15	Phantom V	5 LBX 88	7 passenger Limousine	
9032	PV 15	Phantom V	5 CG 5	7 passenger Limousine	Narrow wheel arches
9033	PV 15	Phantom V	5 LCG 25	7 passenger Limousine	Geneva Show 1962
9035	PV 15	Phantom V	5 BX 42	7 passenger Limousine	
9036	PV 15	Phantom V	5 LVA 11	7 passenger Limousine	
9037	PV 15	Phantom V	5 CG 43	7 passenger Limousine	
9038	PV 15	Phantom V	5 LVA 3	7 passenger Limousine	Earls Court Show 1962
9039	PV 15	Phantom V	5 VA 77	7 passenger Limousine	
9040	PV 15	Phantom V	5 LVA 69	7 passenger Limousine	
9041	PV 15	Phantom V	5 LVA 85	7 passenger Limousine	
9042	PV 15	Phantom V	5 LVA 107	7 passenger Limousine	
9043	PV 15	Phantom V	5 LVB 23	7 passenger Limousine	
9044	PV 15	Phantom V	5 VB 45	7 passenger Limousine	
9045	PV 15	Phantom V	5 LVC 33	7 passenger Limousine	
9046	PV 15	Phantom V	5 LVC 21	7 passenger Limousine	
9047	PV 15	Phantom V	5 LVD 21	7 passenger Limousine	
9048	PV 15	Phantom V	5 VD 71	7 passenger Limousine	
9049	PV 15	Phantom V	5 VD 93	7 passenger Saloon	No division
9050	PV 15	Phantom V	5 LVD 79	7 passenger Limousine	
9051	PV 15	Phantom V	5 LVD 31	7 passenger Limousine	
9052	PV 15	Phantom V	5 LVD 33	7 passenger Limousine	Special quarter light and back light
9053	PV 15	Phantom V	5 VE 21	7 passenger Sedanca de Ville	Earls Court Show 1965
9054	PV 16	Phantom V	5 VE 47	7 passenger Limousine	

JOB NO	DESIGN NO	CHASSIS	CHASSIS NO	TYPE OF BODY	REMARKS
9055	PV 16	Phantom V	5 LVF 33	7 passenger Limousine	
9056	PV 16	Phantom V	5 VF 9	7 passenger Limousine	
9057	PV 16	Phantom V	5 LVF 41	7 passenger Limousine	
9058	PV 16	Phantom V	5 VF 73	7 passenger Limousine	
9059	PV 16	Phantom V		7 passenger Limousine	
9060	PV 16	Phantom V	5 VF 53	7 passenger Saloon	No division
9100	PV 22	Phantom V	5 LAS 1	Touring Limousine	Paris Salon 1959
9101	PV 22	Phantom V	5 LAS 11	Touring Limousine	Earls Court Show 1959
9102	PV 22	Phantom V	5 LAS 35	Touring Limousine	Geneva Show 1960
9103	PV 22	Phantom V	5 AS 9	Touring Limousine	R.R. Stand, Earls Court Show 1959
9104	PV 22	Phantom V	5 AS 41	Touring Limousine	
9105	PV 22	Phantom V	5 LAS 51	Touring Limousine	
9106	PV 22	Phantom V	5 AS 49	Touring Limousine	
9107	PV 22	Phantom V	5 AS 65	Touring Limousine	
9108	PV 22 SD	Phantom V	5 AS 95	Sedanca de Ville	
9109	PV 22	Phantom V	5 AT 100	Touring Limousine	
9110	PV 22 MB	Phantom V	5 LAS 25	Touring Limousine	Special boot
9111	PV 22 SD	Phantom V	5 AT 8	Sedanca de Ville	Earls Court Show 1960
9112	PV 22	Phantom V	5 AS 97	Touring Limousine	
9113	PV 22	Phantom V	5 LAT 44	Touring Limousine	
9116	PV 55	Phantom V	5 LBV 69	2 door Touring Limousine	
9117	PV 22 SD	Phantom V	5 AT 76	Sedanca de Ville	
9118	PV 22 SD	Phantom V	5 LBV 23	Sedanca de Ville	Geneva Show 1961
9119	PV 22	Phantom V	5 BV 29	Touring Limousine	
9120	PV 22	Phantom V	5 BV 17	Touring Limousine	
9121	PV 22	Phantom V	5 BV 79	Touring Limousine	
9122	PV 22 SD	Phantom V	5 LBV 23	Sedanca de Ville	
9123	PV 22	Phantom V	5 LBV 27	Touring Limousine	
9124	PV 22	Phantom V	5 LBV 3	Touring Limousine	
9125	PV 22	Phantom V	5 BX 18	Touring Limousine	
9126	PV 22	Phantom V	5 LAT 26	Touring Limousine	
9127	PV 22	Phantom V	5 BV 99	Touring Limousine	
9128	PV 22	Phantom V	5 BX 8	Saloon	
9129	PV 22	Phantom V	5 BX 22	Touring Limousine	
9130	PV 22	Phantom V	5 BX 38	Touring Limousine	
9131	PV 22	Phantom V	5 LBX 24	Touring Limousine	
9132	PV 22	Phantom V	5 LBX 2	Touring Limousine	
9133	PV 22	Phantom V	5 BX 16	Touring Limousine	
9134	PV 22	Phantom V	5 BX 34	Touring Limousine	
9136	PV 22	Phantom V	5 LBX 40	Touring Limousine	Paris Salon 1961
9137	PV 22	Phantom V	5 LBX 72	Touring Limousine	
9138	PV 22	Phantom V	5 BX 52	Touring Limousine	Earls Court Show 1961
9139	PV 22	Phantom V	5 LBX 74	Touring Limousine	
9140	PV 22 SD	Phantom V	5 BX 44	Sedanca de Ville	
9141	PV 22	Phantom V	5 LBX 76	Touring Limousine	2 door
9142	PV 22	Phantom V	5 BX 80	Touring Limousine	
9143	PV 22	Phantom V	5 BX 86	Touring Limousine	Small backlight
9144	PV 22	Phantom V	5 BX 98	Touring Limousine	
9145	PV 22	Phantom V	5 CG 7	Touring Limousine	
9146	PV 22	Phantom V	5 CG 35	Touring Limousine	
9147	PV 22	Phantom V	5 LCG 19	Touring Limousine	
9149	PV 22	Phantom V	5 LCG 75	Touring Limousine	

JAMES YOUNG

JOB NO	DESIGN NO	CHASSIS	CHASSIS NO	TYPE OF BODY	REMARKS
9150	PV 22	Phantom V	5 CG 69	Touring Limousine	
9151	PV 22	Phantom V	5 LCG 45	Touring Limousine	New York Show 1962
9152	PV 22	Phantom V	5 LCG 67	Touring Limousine	
9154	PV 22	Phantom V	5 LCG 73	Touring Limousine	
9155	PV 22	Phantom V	5 VA 7	Touring Limousine	Earls Court Show 1962
9156	PV 22	Phantom V	5 LVA 1	Touring Limousine	Paris Salon 1962,
9158	PV 22	Phantom V	5 LCG 77	Touring Limousine	
9159	PV 22	Phantom V	5 VA 17	Touring Limousine	
9160	PV 22	Phantom V	5 LVA 43	Touring Limousine	
9161	PV 22	Phantom V	5 LVA 41	Touring Limousine	
9162	PV 22	Phantom V	5 LVA 19	Touring Limousine	
9163	PV 22	Phantom V	5 VA 47	Touring Limousine	
9164	PV 22	Phantom V	5 LVA 49	Touring Limousine	
9165	PV 22	Phantom V	5 LVA 51	Touring Limousine	
9166	PV 22	Phantom V	5 LVA 53	Saloon	
9167	PV 22	Phantom V	5 LVA 55	Touring Limousine	
9168	PV 22	Phantom V	5 VA 61	Touring Limousine	Geneva Show 1963
9169	PV 22	Phantom V	5 VA 63	Touring Limousine	
9170	PV 22	Phantom V	5 LVA 73	Touring Limousine	
9171	PV 22	Phantom V	5 LVA 99	Touring Limousine	
9172	PV 22	Phantom V	5 LVA 103	Touring Limousine	
9173	PV 22	Phantom V	5 LVA 105	Saloon	
9174	PV 22	Phantom V	5 LVA 91	Touring Limousine	
9175	PV 22	Phantom V	5 VA 89	Touring Limousine	
9176	PV 22	Phantom V	5 LVA 113	Touring Limousine	
9177	PV 22	Phantom V	5 VA 119	Touring Limousine	
9178	PV 22	Phantom V	5 VB 3	Touring Limousine	
9179	PV 22	Phantom V	5 VB 5	Touring Limousine	
9180	PV 22	Phantom V	5 LVA 121	Touring Limousine	Paris Salon 1963
9181	PV 22	Phantom V	5 VB 1	Touring Limousine	Earls Court Show 1963
9182	PV 22	Phantom V	5 LVA 123	Touring Limousine	
9183	PV 22	Phantom V	5 LVB 7	Touring Limousine	
9184	PV 22	Phantom V	5 VB 15	Touring Limousine	
9185	PV 22	Phantom V	5 LVB 19	Touring Limousine	
9186	PV 22	Phantom V	5 VB 21	Touring Limousine	
9187	PV 22	Phantom V	5 VB 27	Touring Limousine	
9188	PV 22	Phantom V	5 VB 31	Touring Limousine	
9189	PV 22	Phantom V	5 LVB 41	Touring Limousine	
9190	PV 22	Phantom V	5 VC 7	Touring Limousine	
9191	PV 22	Phantom V	5 LVB 49	Touring Limousine	New York Show
9192	PV 22	Phantom V	5 VC 15	Touring Limousine	
9193	PV 22	Phantom V	5 LVC 3	Touring Limousine	
9194	PV 22	Phantom V	5 VC 17	Touring Limousine	
9195	PV 22	Phantom V	5 LVC 9	Touring Limousine	
9196	PV 22	Phantom V	5 VC 43	Touring Limousine	
9197	PV 22	Phantom V	5 LVC 31	Touring Limousine	
9198	PV 22	Phantom V	5 LVC 51	Touring Limousine	
9199	PV 22	Phantom V	5 VC 41	Touring Limousine	
9200	PV 22	Phantom V	5 VD 3	Touring Limousine	
9201	PV 22	Phantom V	5 VD 5	Touring Limousine	
9202	PV 22	Phantom V	5 VD 17	Touring Limousine	Earls Court Show 1964
9203	PV 22	Phantom V	5 VD 11	Touring Limousine	

JOB NO	DESIGN NO	CHASSIS	CHASSIS NO	TYPE OF BODY	REMARKS
9204	PV 22	Phantom V	5 VD 37	Touring Limousine	
9205	PV 22	Phantom V	5 LVD 29	Touring Limousine	No quarter lights
9206	PV 22	Phantom V	5 VD 25	Touring Limousine	
9207	PV 22	Phantom V	5 VD 53	Touring Limousine	
9208	PV 22	Phantom V	5 VD 55	Touring Limousine	
9209	PV 22	Phantom V	5 LVD 43	Touring Limousine	
9210	PV 22	Phantom V	5 VD 59	Touring Limousine	
9211	PV 22	Phantom V	5 LVD 67	Touring Limousine	Geneva Show 1965
9212	PV 22	Phantom V	5 LVD 61	Touring Limousine	
9213	PV 22	Phantom V	5 VD 75	Touring Limousine	
9215	PV 22	Phantom V	5 VD 89	Touring Limousine	
9216	PV 22	Phantom V	5 LVD 97	Touring Limousine	
9217	PV 22	Phantom V	5 VE 11	Touring Limousine	
9218	PV 23	Phantom V	5 VE 25	Touring Limousine	
9219	PV22SDM	Phantom V	5 VE 1	Sedanca de Ville	Special quarter lights
9220	PV 23	Phantom V	5 LVE 27	Touring Limousine	
9221	PV 23	Phantom V	5 VE 51	Touring Limousine	
9222	PV 23	Phantom V	5 LVE 23	Touring Limousine	Earls Court Show 1965
9223	PV 23	Phantom V	5 VF 1	Touring Limousine	
9224	PV 22 S	Phantom V	5 LVE 29	Saloon	
9225	PV 23	Phantom V	5 LVE 49	Touring Limousine	
9226	PV 23	Phantom V	5 VF 11	Touring Limousine	
9227	PV 23	Phantom V	5 LVF 3	Touring Limousine	Geneva Show 1966
9228	PV 23	Phantom V	5 VF 21	Touring Limousine	
9229	PV 23	Phantom V	5 VF 37	Touring Limousine	
9230	PV 23	Phantom V	5 LVF 45	Touring Limousine	
9231	PV 23	Phantom V	5 LVF 49	Touring Limousine	P100 headlights

The James Young stand at Earls Court in October 1948.

A Saloon Coupé, design WR 16, on a Silver Wraith chassis.

Below: Silver Wraith, WZB 57 with four door Sports Saloon, design WR 17, the first post war model.

Two views of four door Saloon, registration No. KLO 1, a very early design WR 18, which is a more rounded version of design WR 17.

Silver Wraith, WCB 20 with Saloon body, design WR 18, probably a James Young show car at Earls Court 1948.

Below: with Alligator Boot, design WR 18, on a Silver Wraith chassis.

Drop-head Coupé, design WR 20, on a Silver Wraith chassis, built for the Maharajah of Mysore.

Below: a similar car, showing the hood folded and stowed. Design WR 20 was mainly, if not solely, made at the Gurney Nutting factory and an example exhibited on the Gurney Nutting stand at Earls Court in 1948, presumably as a Gurney Nutting body.

Two photographs of a Drop-head Coupe on a Silver Wraith chassis, also apparently design WR 20, as this was the only James Young Drop-head Coupé design at that time. It is very similar to the previous page cars except for the boot and the scuttle ventilators.

Another illustration of design WR 18, this time on Silver Wraith, WCB 46, and below: to show how subtle changes in line vastly improve the overall effect is design WR 19, a four door Sports Saloon. The raising of the wing line and the slight lengthening and raking of the boot has made a long elegant car out of the previous chunky design.

Two Silver Dawns with design C20SD, four door four light Saloon bodies, the upper with a modified boot and rear wing.

Three views of design WR 25, a four door Sports Saloon on a Silver Wraith chassis, this car is the James Young stand show car of 1950.

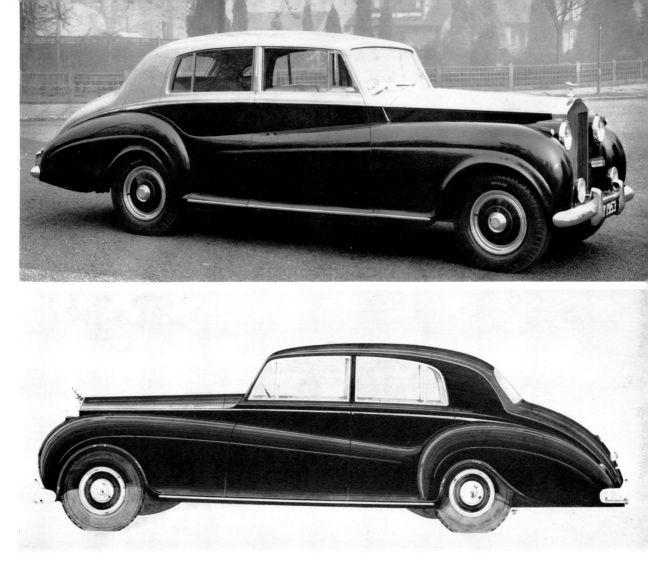

Design No. WR 26, four door saloon on a Silver Wraith chassis.

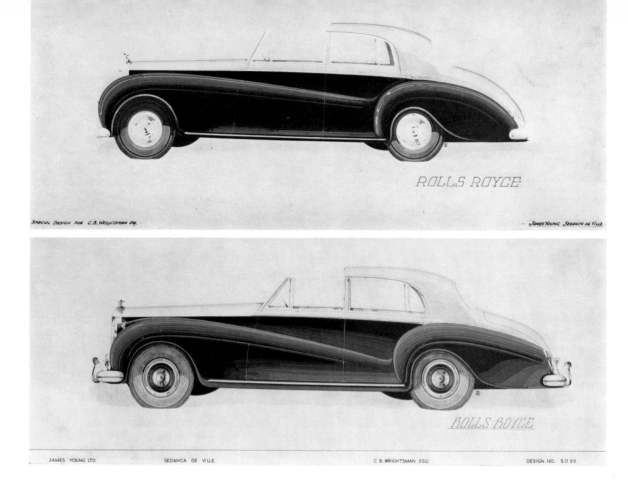

ROLLS ROYCE

SPECIAL DESIGN FOR C.B.WRIGHTSMAN Eq. — JAMES YOUNG, SEDANCA DE VILLE

JAMES YOUNG LTD.   SEDANCA DE VILLE.   C.B.WRIGHTSMAN. ESQ.   DESIGN. NO. S.D.29.

Two special designs for C. B. Wrightsman Esq., for Sedanca de Villes, the top design presumably for a Silver Wraith chassis the lower design for a Silver Dawn.

The drawing below although captioned 'Design SW11', I believe to be design SW 10, which is a design WRM 31, with a modified boot, of which four bodies were made.

JAMES YOUNG LTD.   SALOON WITH DIVISION   SILVER WRAITH DESIGN S.W.11.

Four Door Saloon with division, design WRM 30, on a Silver Wraith chassis. This design is very similar to design WRM 31 shown on the next page, but note the double swaging on the front and rear wings against the single swaging on design WRM 31.

Design WRM 31, four door Saloon on a Silver Wraith chassis. This is an early example of this design with WRM 30 rear wing ends and rear lights.

Two more of WRM 31 design, later cars than the above version with the modified rear wings to take the modern light cluster.

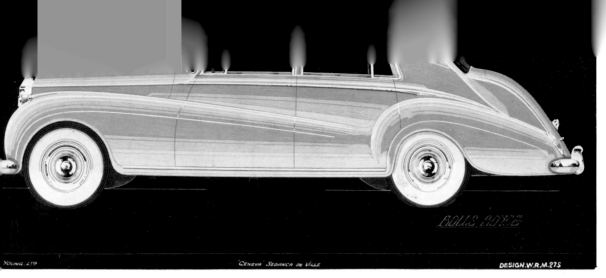

Design WRM 27, a Sedanca de Ville version of design WRM 31. The above drawing entitled 'Geneva Sedanca de Ville' obviously refers to Job No. 1864 on Silver Wraith, ELW 44, which was shown at the Geneva show in 1956.

Design WRM 27 early and late, the above car is without normally positioned sidelights and with old style rear wings, rear lights and overriders.

Seven passenger Touring Limousine, design WRM 35S, on a Silver Wraith chassis. Its affiliation to WRM 31 is obvious, externally it appears to be the same up to the rear edge of the rear door. The interior is suitably luxurious with radio knobs and buttons and a smoking companion to keep the near side rear passenger busy and happy.

Wash and line drawings with dimensions of WRM 35S.

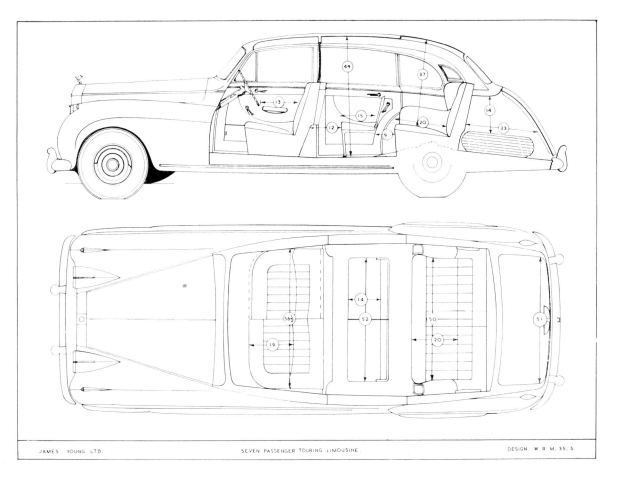

JAMES YOUNG LTD.   SEVEN PASSENGER TOURING LIMOUSINE.   DESIGN. W. R. M. 35. S.

JAMES YOUNG LTD.   FOUR DOOR SPORTS SALOON.   DESIGN S.C.10

The first of the James Young Silver Clouds. Design SC 10, termed a four door Sports Saloon. The early cars of this design sported a thin fin on the rear wings.

Still Design SC 10, but the fin has vanished.

Below: Silver Cloud, SXA 129, body No. 4010, with enlarged rear window, small louvres in the rear panel and a rather cumbersome headlamp treatment.

JAMES YOUNG Lᵀᴰ   FOUR DOOR SPORTS SALOON.   DESIGN S.C. 10. S.

A very handsome 2 door Drop-head Coupé version of design SC 10. This car is either body No. 4029 or 4031 having a left-hand driving position.

More photographs of the same car showing, above: the disappearing quarter light with the hood still raised, and below: with hood lowered and stowed.

Silver Cloud with Sedanca Coupé body.

The wash drawing calls it a Sedanca Coupé, design SC 23, but reference to the Body Book will show no such number, it appears to be a Sedanca version of the SC 10 design with modified wing treatment.

JAMES YOUNG

On the opposite page are three designs based on the SC 10 design, they are from top to bottom: 2 door Saloon Coupé, design SC 20, Sedanca Coupé, design SC 22D and Sedanca de Ville, design SC 50D.

Above: a wash drawing of design SC 12, this is a long wheelbase version of SC 10. Below: is Silver Cloud, BLC 15, body No. 4060, design SC 12 which was exhibited at Earls Court in 1958.

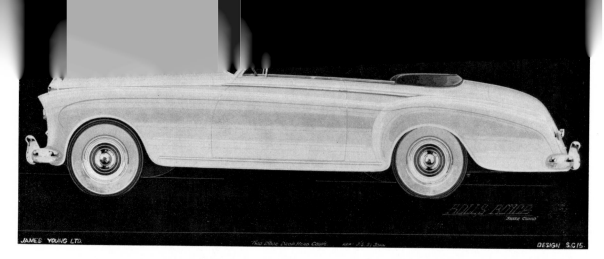

Three more McNeil design drawings, a 2 door Drop-head Coupé, design SC 15, a 2 seater Coupé, design SC 25 SM and a 2 door Saloon Coupé, design SC 70. I can find no trace of any of these cars having been built.

The very elegant SCT 100 design on Silver Clouds II and III, Long Wheelbase. The line drawing is incorrect as it shows the doors hinged front and rear whereas they are in fact hinged at the front. The top car is Silver Cloud II, LCB 7, exhibited at Earls Court in 1960 and the bottom car is Silver Cloud III, CAL 3, exhibited at Earls Court in 1962.

JAMES YOUNG LTD.   DESIGN. S.C.T. 100.

JAMES YOUNG

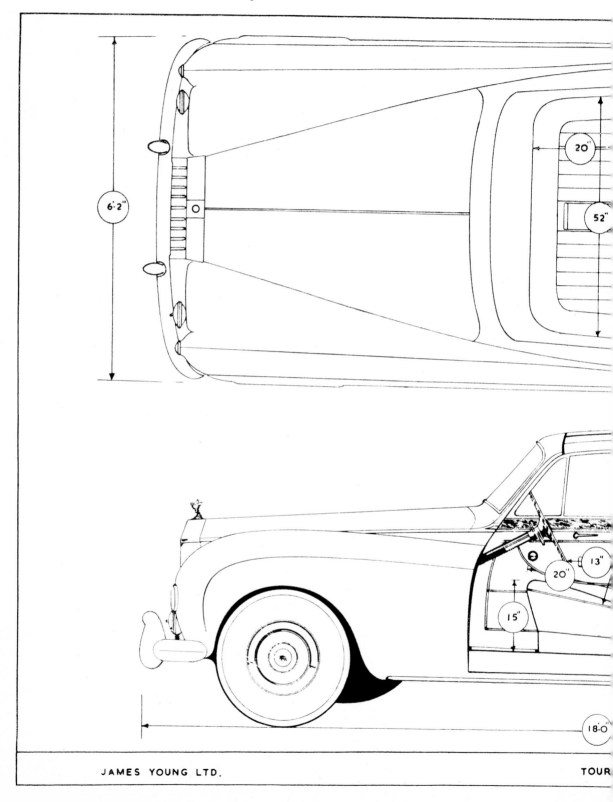

TOUR

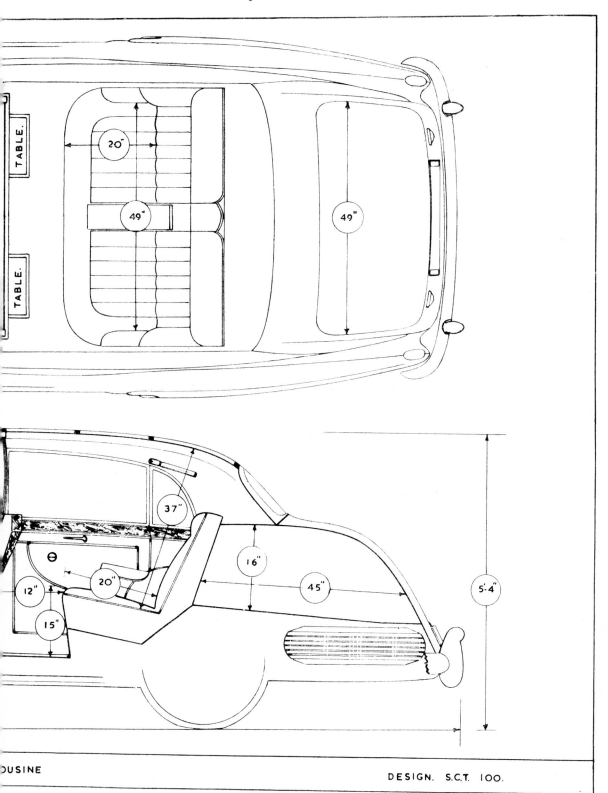

TABLE.

TABLE.

Body No. 4168, design SCT 200, a Saloon-Coupé on Silver Cloud III, LCDL 1, supplied to the King of Morocco.

Standard wheelbase Silver Cloud III, design SCV 100, sometimes referred to as a James Young Flying Spur.

Below: is the two door version, this car being chassis No. SGT 609C, which was exhibited at the 1964 Earls Court show.

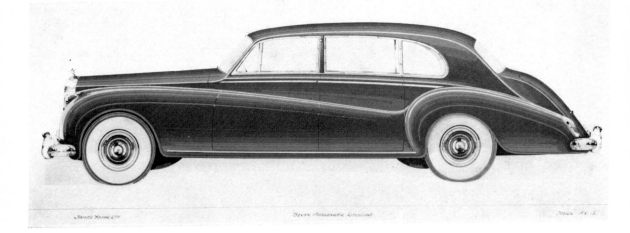

It was on the Phantom V chassis that James Young found their peak of elegance, although design No. PV 15, a seven passenger Limousine, did not allow the full scope due to the necessity of seating so many people in comfort within a given wheelbase.

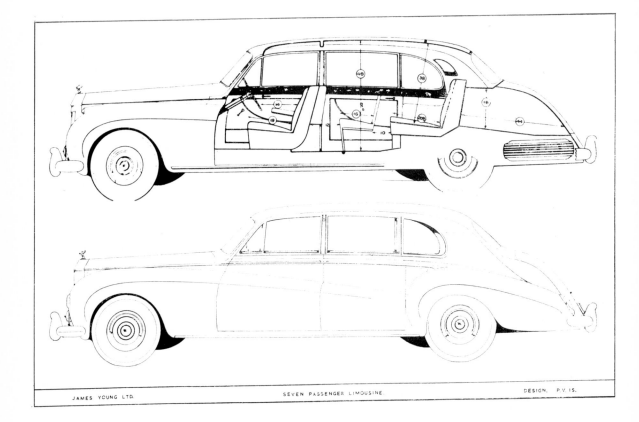

JAMES YOUNG LTD.   SEVEN PASSENGER LIMOUSINE.   DESIGN. P.V. 15.

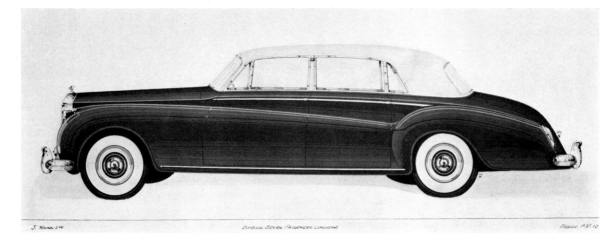

Variations on the PV 15 theme, design PV 10, with a much smaller rear quarter light and a longer boot, design PV 15 SD, with a Sedanca de Ville front and design PV 16, with a Hooper style rear quarter light.

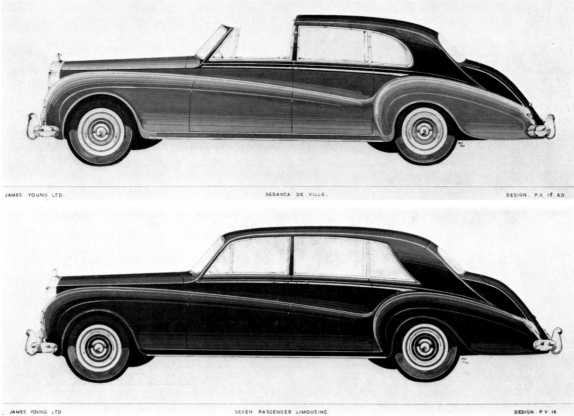

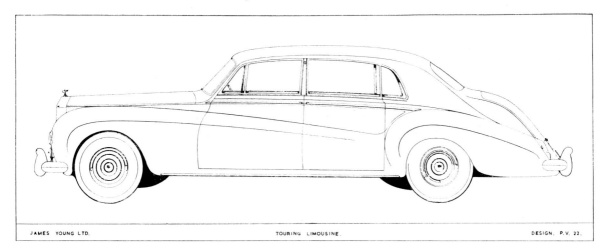

JAMES YOUNG LTD.   TOURING LIMOUSINE.   DESIGN. P.V. 22.

Design PV 22, a Touring Limousine on the Phantom V chassis. Compare the above drawing with the similar drawing of design SCT 100. The extra 17 inches the Phantom V has in its wheelbase makes possible design PV 22's steeply raked back, larger boot and generally more sweeping lines, thus decreasing the impression of height. The bottom drawing is of PV 22 SD, a Sedanca de Ville version of PV 22.

JAMES YOUNG LTD.   TOURING LIMOUSINE.   DESIGN. P.V. 22.

JAMES YOUNG LTD.   SEDANCA DE VILLE, FOR L. T. LOCAN, ESQ.   DESIGN. P.V. 22. S.D.

Magnificence inside to match the elegance outside. Three views and an interior shot of design PV 22.

Design PV 22SD, the Sedanca de Ville version of design PV 22, an oft-used photograph.

JAMES YOUNG LTD.   TOURING LIMOUSINE.   DESIGN   P. V. 22. M.R.

Touring Limousine, design PV 22 MR.
Below: with an unhappy roof/boot line is presumably design PV 55, although the Body Book
calls it a two door.

Design PV 23, a later modification of PV 22, the only obvious difference being the Hooper style quarter light.

Below: wash drawings of PV 23 and PV 23 SD, the Sedanca de Ville version of PV 23.

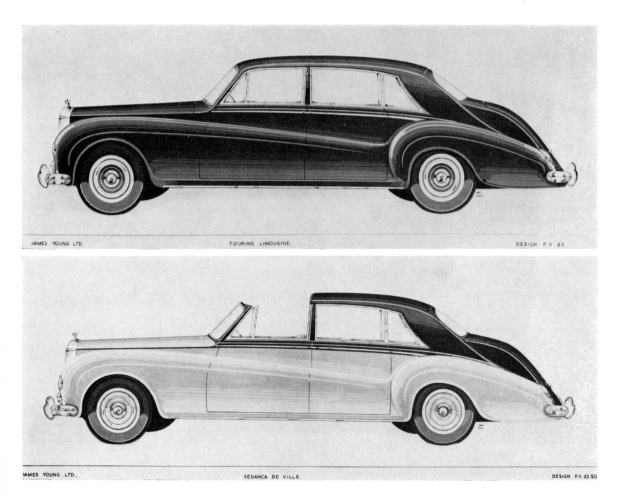

JAMES YOUNG LTD.   TOURING LIMOUSINE.   DESIGN P.V 23

JAMES YOUNG . LTD.,   SEDANCA DE VILLE.   DESIGN. P.V. 23. SD

JAMES YOUNG LTD.,   TWO DOOR SALOON. SILVER SHADOW   S.Y. 150.

Design SY 150, a two door Saloon which is in fact a modified standard four door Saloon. Fifty cars of the design were made, some having Bentley radiators, before James Young ceased coachbuilding in 1967.

CHAPTER EIGHT

FROM CHAPRON TO WINDOVERS

In this chapter are gathered together the foreign coachbuilders, who only ever made a few bodies for Rolls-Royce, the English coachbuilders who survived the war but ceased building bodies within five or six years and only constructed a relatively small number of bodies and the few small coachbuilders who either modified standard steel saloons or built but one or two bodies. Work of the following coachbuilders is illustrated.

HENRI CHAPRON	F. L. M. PANELCRAFT
PININ FARINA	HAROLD RADFORD
FRANAY	RIPPON
GHIA	SAOUTCHIK
GURNEY NUTTING	VIGNALE
HARWOOD	VINCENTS OF READING
INSKIP	WINDOVERS
GUSTAF NORDBERGS	

A French body with an English soul is an apt description of this Phantom V's coachwork. Ordered by Mr. Marty Martyn just as Hoopers ceased production, this body was designed by Mr. Osmond Rivers of Hoopers and built by Henri Chapron of Paris under Mr. Rivers supervision.

The design followed the later Hooper designs and is very similar to design No. 8585.
The interior has a light and airy look.

Two photographs of the Pinin Farina two door Saloon on a Silver Dawn chassis, which was exhibited at the Turin Show in 1951.

The Gurney Nutting stand at Earls Court in 1948.
Note the Silver Wraith at the extreme right and then turn to page 212.
Below is Silver Wraith WDC 8, with a Fixed-head Coupé body by Gurney Nutting.

FRANAY

A Limousine de Ville by Franay on a Silver Wraith chassis, which was exhibited at the Paris Salon in 1952. Painted in primrose and grey, it was, at £8000, the most expensive car at the Show and was purchased by the King of Iraq.

Silver Wraith, WYA 69 with a Franay Drop-head Coupé body, owned by Dr Irving Thrasher.

Silver Wraith, WYA 75 with a Saloon body by Harwood Coachworks, at present owned by T. H. Baker Esq.

A Ghia Limousine bodied Silver Dawn winning the Grand Prix d'Honneur at the Villa Borghese, Rome in 1952, This car with a lengthened and lowered bonnet was exhibited at the 1952 Turin Show.

An Inskip Custom Convertible on Silver Wraith, WZB 36, owned by Andrew Darling Esq.

A Silver Cloud standard steel Saloon much modified by F. L. M. Panelcraft of London for Nubar Gulbenkian Esq., and converted into a Sedanca de Ville with altered rear quarter lights and hooded head and tail lamps.

A very Parisian conception of a Sedanca Coupé by Saoutchik on Silver Wraith, WTA 45.

HAROLD RADFORD

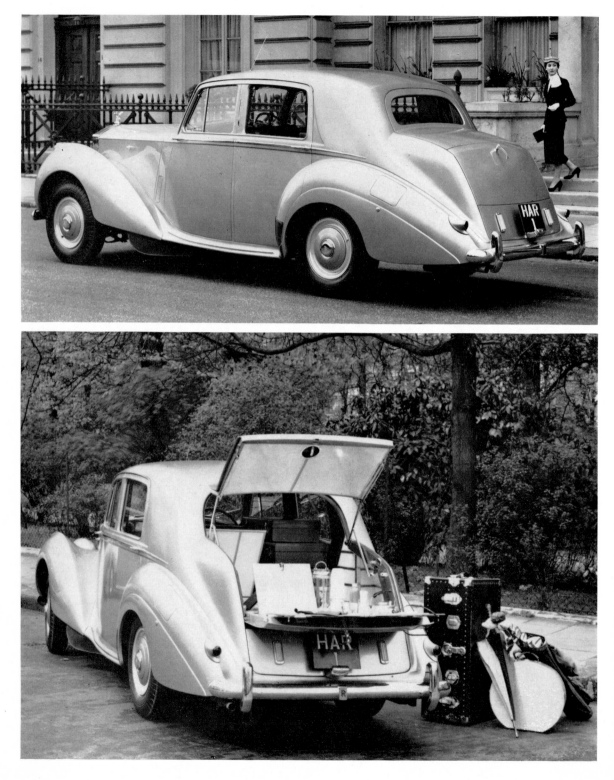

Four photographs of a Silver Dawn standard steel Saloon modified by Harold Radford (Coachbuilders) Ltd. as a Countryman Saloon.

The Silver Wraith exhibited at Earls Court in 1950 by Rippon Bros. was termed a Continental Touring Saloon.

Detail of the excellent workmanship in the above car. The 'Autocar' in its review of the 1950 Motor Show wrote 'Every joint was perfection'.

Above: the 1952 Earls Court Show car, a Sports Saloon without division on a Silver Wraith chassis, and below, presumably by the higher wing line, a later body, also on a Silver Wraith chassis.

The *Vincents of Reading* 1949 *Earls Court Show car, a Silver Wraith Saloon complete with fitted suitcases and a roller blind type of dust cover, the lid of the boot may be used as a luggage platform.*

For the 1951 show, Vincents concealed the running boards. The show Saloon pictured above is a Silver Wraith, WOF 1

Below are Silver Wraith, WVA 62, a 7 passenger Limousine and at the bottom another Limousine this time on Silver Wraith, WTA 40, also owned by G. W. Harris, Esq.

Windovers only built four bodies for post-war Rolls-Royce chassis, three of design No. 135 above and one of the design below.

Above is the first post-war Windovers Rolls-Royce body on Silver Wraith, WTA 80, registration No. JLM 455, owned by Chiltern Cars Ltd., and below is the last Windovers Rolls-Royce body built, a Saloon on Silver Wraith, WCB 9, at present owned by A. C. Bell, Esq.

The Saloon pictured above is by Vignale on a Silver Wraith chassis. The other two illustrations depict a Saloon by Gustaf Nordbergs of Stockholm mounted on a Silver Wraith chassis in 1954.

HOOPER & CO. (COACHBUILDERS) LTD. LONDON

COACHWORK BY JAMES YOUNG LTD BROMLEY KENT

CHISWICK H.J. Mulliner & Co., Ltd. LONDON

Park-Ward Coachwork

FREESTONE & WEBB LTD
101-103, BRENTFIELD ROAD, WILLESDEN, N.W. 10. ELGAR 6671·2·3

COACHWORK BY
H.J. Mulliner, Park Ward Limited.
WILLESDEN LONDON